DOWNTIME DISASTERS: WHEN EVERYTHING THAT CAN GO WRONG, DOES

A JOURNEY THROUGH THE CHAOS AND HUMOR OF TECH

By Diwesh Saxena

"Because in the world of tech, disaster is inevitable—but so is recovery."

PREFACE

In the world of technology, there's a saying that has echoed through the halls of every office, startup, and server room: "Anything that can go wrong, will go wrong." It's a phrase that captures the very essence of life in tech, where systems crash, bugs emerge, and even the simplest tasks can spiral into full-blown crisis. As a CTO, I've lived this reality day in and day out, and it's from this ever-chaotic world that this book was born.

"Downtime Disasters: When Everything That Can Go Wrong, Does" is not just a collection of war stories, but a reflection on the unique combination of chaos, humor, and resilience that defines the life of a tech leader. Each chapter dives into a disaster or challenge—whether it's a system crash that brings the company to its knees, an overnight bug hunt that leaves the team running on fumes, or the endless cycle of patches and updates that never seem to end.

But more than the disasters themselves, this book is about how we respond to them. It's about the human element —how a team comes together to solve problems, how a leader stays calm in the storm, and how humor and optimism can turn even the most frustrating moments into opportunities for growth.

In writing this book, I wanted to capture the lighthearted yet gritty reality of life in tech. There's no sugarcoating here—things will go wrong, often at the worst possible moment. But through every crash, every bug, and every endless update, there's something valuable to be learned. And, in hindsight, some of those disasters make for pretty entertaining stories.

This book is for anyone who's been through the trenches of technology, for every developer who's stayed up all night chasing a bug, for every project manager who's juggled an ever-growing list of client demands, and for every leader who's watched their carefully planned sprint get derailed by an unexpected outage. Whether you're just starting your career or you've been around long enough to have a few grey hairs courtesy of those all-too-familiar late-night emergencies, I hope this book brings a smile to your face—and maybe even helps you see the humor in your next disaster.

Because in the end, tech isn't just about solving problems. It's about embracing the chaos, leading through it, and finding growth in every challenge that comes your way.

— Diwesh Saxena

TABLE OF CONTENTS

caused the entire crash.

8. **The Stress Fueled by Caffeine (and Panic)**
How the team survives on nothing but coffee, adrenaline, and blind optimism.

9. **The Client Who Wants Updates Every Five Minutes**
Juggling a system meltdown and constant client requests for status updates.

10. **The Phantom Bug That Disappears**
The mysterious bug that vanishes without a trace—just as suddenly as it appeared.

11. **The Hero Developer**
The unsung hero who swoops in to save the day while everyone else panics.

12. **The Aftermath: Postmortems and Blame Games**
Picking up the pieces and figuring out who (or what) is responsible.

13. **The Fix That Breaks Everything Else**
When the solution creates even bigger problems.

14. **The Client Celebration, CTO's Internal Screams**
The paradox of client satisfaction versus the team's utter exhaustion.

15. **The Team Finally Sleeps...Until the Next Call**
The well-deserved break that's always too short.

16. **Recurring Nightmares of the CTO**

The mental trauma that comes with every downtime disaster.

17. **Lessons from the Chaos**

The "lessons learned" meetings where everyone swears it won't happen again. (It will.)

18. **Automate Everything (But Nobody Understands the Code)**

The challenges of automating solutions and why it's not always the perfect fix.

19. **That One Person Who Missed the Entire Crisis**

The lucky soul who wakes up fresh and clueless after the storm has passed.

20. **And Then the Wi-Fi Really Does Go Down**

Ending with the irony of real-life technical failures.

CHAPTER 1: THE 2 AM CALL

There's an unwritten rule in the world of technology: **systems only crash at 2 AM**. Never 2 PM when you're wide awake and sipping coffee. Nope, it's 2 AM when you're comfortably nestled in bed, dreaming of a problem-free world where servers don't crash, code behaves, and databases never go down.

But of course, that's not the world we live in.

Your phone buzzes. At first, you think it's an alarm. Maybe a reminder to turn off the lights. But then it buzzes again. And again. This isn't a gentle wake-up call—this is a system emergency. You sit up in bed, already knowing what's coming before you even check your phone.

There it is: **"URGENT: Site down. Major outage. Need everyone online."**

It's the kind of message that sends a jolt of adrenaline through your system. Your sleep-deprived brain might be foggy, but you know it's go time. But instead of panicking, you take a deep breath. As CTO, you've been here before, and you'll be here again. **Crisis? Or opportunity? Let's find out.**

WAKING UP WITH A SMILE (SORT OF)

Rolling out of bed, you manage to grab your laptop without tripping over anything (a small victory at 2 AM). You consider grabbing a coffee but decide against it—caffeine at this hour might make you jittery. Plus, this isn't your first rodeo. You know that staying calm, focused, and, yes, **humorous** is the best way to lead your team through chaos.

You log in, check Slack, and see that your team is already online, trying to make sense of the situation. The messages are pouring in fast:

> **"Can't access the database. Is it just me?"**

> **"I think the server crashed. Or maybe the cloud just left us?"**

> **"Why does this always happen at night?"**

You chuckle, because deep down, you know the only way through this is to keep the mood light. There's no need for blame, no time for panic. **Let's**

fix this and grow from it.

RALLYING THE TROOPS (VIRTUALLY)

You jump into the conversation with a quick message:

> **"Alright, team. Let's stay calm and take it step by step. First one to solve it gets free coffee for a week."**

There's a round of virtual laughter (at least, that's how you imagine it). And just like that, the team's spirits are lifted. Everyone's still half-asleep, but now they're a half-asleep team with a mission— and maybe some humor-fueled energy.

First up, check the basics: **server status, database connections, error logs**. It's a familiar dance, one that you've done many times before. But each time, you know you're sharpening the team's ability to problem-solve under pressure.

THE WI-FI IS ALWAYS GUILTY (UNTIL PROVEN INNOCENT)

Now, you'd think after all these years, the **Wi-Fi** would get tired of being blamed for every tech problem. But here we are, checking it first, because there's always that faint hope that rebooting the router will magically solve everything.

But alas, the Wi-Fi's innocent this time. Moving on.

> **"Wi-Fi's fine, folks. It's something deeper. Let's dig in."**

One of the devs suggests a potential issue with the server configuration. Another throws out the possibility that it's a database problem. You love seeing this—everyone's throwing out ideas, **engaged** and ready to tackle the challenge. This is what leadership is about: **empowering your team to problem-solve together**.

THE COFFEE BREAK THAT NEVER HAPPENS

Half an hour in, you feel that familiar temptation to grab a coffee. But you resist, because you know the **moment you leave your desk**, something will happen. It's a universal truth in tech: **the second you're not looking, the problem magically reveals itself**. It's like the system knows.

And you were right. Because just as you contemplate sneaking to the kitchen for a cup of joe, one of your devs chimes in:

> **"I think I found it. There's a missing connection in the database. It's fixable, but it might take a few minutes."**

Ah, the moment of hope. You knew it would come. But rather than rushing to solve it, you smile and give your team the encouragement they need:

> **"Awesome work. Take your time, no rush. We've got this under control."**

Because the secret to leadership in crisis mode isn't solving everything yourself—it's **trusting your team to step up and learn from the process**. They're handling it, and you're there to guide them.

IT'S FIXED...
ALMOST

After what feels like an eternity (but is really just 20 minutes), the system comes back online. The site breathes again, the database connection is restored, and everything is functioning as it should. It's a small victory, but a victory nonetheless.

The team celebrates in Slack with a round of funny GIFs, because in moments like these, humor is how you decompress. You jump in:

"Great work, team! See? We didn't need the coffee after all. Let's remember this one for the next time!"

TURNING CRISIS INTO GROWTH

Sure, crises like these can be stressful, but **it's how you handle them that matters**. Underneath the humor and the late-night adrenaline rush, there's growth happening. The team is learning how to solve problems under pressure, how to communicate effectively, and how to keep things light when they could easily get heavy.

You close out the night with a quick debrief, thanking the team for their effort:

> **"I'm proud of how we handled this. Let's document what we learned and move forward. Great job tonight, everyone. Rest up!"**

It's moments like these that **build a strong team culture**—one based on trust, optimism, and knowing that no matter what comes next, you can face it together.

And maybe next time, you'll actually get that coffee break.

THE OPTIMISTIC TAKEAWAY

So, what did we learn? That crises will always happen, but it's how you approach them that makes the difference. Stay calm, keep your team engaged, and remember that humor can be a powerful tool in leadership.

Because when everything goes wrong, the best leaders know how to keep things right—one laugh, one solution, and one team effort at a time.

CHAPTER 2:
FIRST, BLAME
THE WI-FI

Ah, the **Wi-Fi**. It's the unsung hero and, more often than not, the first scapegoat in any technical crisis. There's something comforting about blaming the Wi-Fi—it's invisible, mysterious, and for some reason, always seems like a plausible culprit. Plus, it's easier to blame something that doesn't have feelings.

It doesn't matter if the servers are in a data center 1,000 miles away or if the issue is buried deep in the code—when the system goes down, our collective brains immediately point to **the Wi-Fi**. After all, it's been sketchy before. Why not now?

This chapter is dedicated to all the times we've furiously restarted routers, only to discover it was something far more complex. But hey, there's something to be said for starting with the simple fixes, right?

STEP 1: REBOOT EVERYTHING!

There's something magical about the **power of the reboot**. Whether it's a server, laptop, or even a router, we've been conditioned to believe that hitting that reboot button is akin to casting a spell. You're not just rebooting a device—you're rebooting hope.

So, naturally, the first thing you do in any tech crisis is check the Wi-Fi. Maybe it's the Wi-Fi, you think. Maybe the router just needs a little nudge.

You glance at the router sitting innocently in the corner, its blinking lights almost mocking you. Still, you get up, walk over, and do the universal ritual: unplug, count to ten, and plug it back in.

You watch as the lights flicker back to life, and for a brief moment, you feel like a tech wizard. Surely, this will fix everything.

THE TEAM FOLLOWS SUIT

While you're rebooting your router, you're certain that somewhere across town (or across the globe), your team members are doing the same thing. Everyone, no matter how senior, has a deep belief in the healing powers of a router reboot. Some say it's **instinct**, others say it's **desperation**, but everyone does it.

And so, you send out a message to the team, half-joking, half-optimistic:

> **"Alright, everyone. Let's start by rebooting routers, just in case. Can't hurt, right?"**

The responses start rolling in.

> **"Already done!"**

> **"Wi-Fi's fine on my end. Must be something deeper."**

> **"I rebooted twice just to be sure. No luck."**

You laugh to yourself, imagining each member of the team performing their own little router dance, only to realize that the problem is far beyond the reach of home networks.

STEP 2: IT'S DEFINITELY NOT THE WI-FI

Once everyone has accepted that the Wi-Fi isn't the root cause, the real work begins. But, if nothing else, the whole process gives the team a chance to ease into the crisis. It's like the warm-up round before the big game.

With the Wi-Fi securely in the clear, you and the team start diving into the **real investigation**: logs, database connections, server statuses. And yet, there's always a moment of nostalgia as you think back to the simplicity of blaming the Wi-Fi. Those were the good times. Now comes the tricky part—**actual problem-solving**.

THE COMFORT OF BLAMING THE SIMPLE THINGS

The thing is, blaming the Wi-Fi gives us a moment of comfort because it offers a quick fix. There's no endless debugging, no deep code analysis, just a simple, satisfying reboot. But when the Wi-Fi is ruled out, it's time to acknowledge that the issue lies somewhere deeper. Somewhere more complex.

As the investigation deepens, you notice the team kicking into high gear. They're no longer rebooting routers; now, they're running queries, testing hypotheses, and combing through logs. And you know what? This is where your team shines.

> **"Okay, team, now that we've ruled out the Wi-Fi, let's see what's really going on. Keep sharing your findings."**

By encouraging the team to communicate, even when the problem seems insurmountable, you're fostering collaboration. Every small discovery adds up. It's like solving a jigsaw puzzle where the pieces are scattered across different devices, and it's your job to help the team fit them together.

FINDING THE REAL CULPRIT

And then it happens—**someone finds the root cause**. It's not glamorous, but there it is: an issue with the database connection. Maybe it was a misconfigured setting, maybe a patch gone awry, or maybe the system just decided to have an existential crisis. But no matter what, your team is on it.

You don't panic. You don't point fingers. Instead, you focus on what matters: **solving the problem together**.

> **"Great work. Now let's get it fixed and back online. We've got this."**

That's all it takes—a little positive reinforcement, a little trust, and a whole lot of teamwork. The issue gets fixed, and the system comes back to life.

The Real Lesson? Always Start with the Simple Stuff

Here's the thing: as much as we laugh about blaming the Wi-Fi, there's a valuable lesson in starting with the **simple fixes**. Sometimes it really is the easy stuff that saves the day (and your sanity). And even when it's not, starting simple gives the team time to organize their thoughts, communicate, and build momentum toward solving the bigger issues.

Plus, let's face it—blaming the Wi-Fi adds a little humor to an otherwise stressful situation. And in the world of tech, humor is a crucial part of keeping morale high, especially during those late-night crisis calls.

TURNING FRUSTRATION INTO GROWTH

Every crisis, no matter how frustrating, is a chance for growth. Each team member learns something new, whether it's a technical skill or the ability to stay calm under pressure. And you, as the leader, learn how to guide them through it.

The next time a crisis hits, your team won't even flinch. They'll know the process: **start with the basics, stay calm, and work together**. And maybe, just maybe, they'll even reboot the Wi-Fi for good measure.

So, what did we learn today? It's not always the Wi-Fi's fault. But it's a good place to start.

THE OPTIMIST'S TAKEAWAY

When a crisis hits, don't overcomplicate things. Start simple, stay calm, and keep the mood light. **Blame the Wi-Fi** if you need to—it gives everyone a moment to breathe and refocus. But when the real work begins, trust your team to rise to the occasion.

Because at the end of the day, it's not just about solving the problem—it's about building a team that knows how to navigate crises with a mix of skill, humor, and optimism.

That wraps up **Chapter 2**! It continues the lighthearted tone while emphasizing teamwork, leadership, and growth. Let me know if you'd like to tweak anything!

CHAPTER 3: CALLING IN THE CAVALRY

It's the middle of the night, and after realizing the **Wi-Fi isn't to blame**, you know what comes next: assembling the team. You could handle this solo, but where's the fun in that? Crisis situations are, after all, a **team-building exercise**—though maybe not the kind you write about in company newsletters.

In moments like these, you realize that being a **CTO** isn't just about managing technology; it's about managing people—sleepy, confused people who are about to dive headfirst into a tech nightmare. You're the **commander** about to call in the cavalry, and you know that your team is somewhere out there, cozy in their beds, blissfully unaware of the impending drama.

But not for long.

THE ART OF THE CRISIS CALL

As CTO, one of the most delicate parts of your job is figuring out **how to wake people up** for an emergency without causing unnecessary panic. There's an art to it—a balance between urgency and reassurance. The trick is not to sound like the sky is falling (even if, deep down, you feel like it is).

You type out the message, carefully crafting it to sound calm and collected, but with just the right amount of "get your butt online ASAP" urgency.

> **"Hey team, slight issue on the live servers. Nothing major, but we need to jump on it now. Let's get online and work through it together."**

Translation: "Everything's on fire, but don't freak out... yet."

You hit send and wait for the responses, hoping that at least one or two members of your team have their phones on loud. There's nothing worse than staring at Slack, watching the **"Seen by no**

one" status, knowing that every minute matters.

SLOWLY, THEY ARRIVE... ONE BY ONE

The first one online is always your **DevOps guy**. He's seen it all before, so nothing rattles him. Within seconds, you get the response you were expecting:

> **"I'm on it. Let's check the logs."**

Next up is your **front-end developer**—the one who insists that every bug looks like a design issue at first glance.

> **"Let me check if it's something with the UI. Not saying it is, but you never know..."**

Then comes the **backend developer**, who's still half-asleep but somehow manages to bring his A-game regardless of the hour.

> **"I was just dreaming about this happening, so I guess I'm ready for it. Where do we start?"**

Finally, your **junior developer** logs in, typing in that dazed, confused manner that suggests they haven't fully accepted the situation.

"Wait, what's going on? Is this a drill?"

And just like that, your team is **assembled**. Some more awake than others, but all ready to tackle the issue head-on. The cavalry has arrived.

LEADERSHIP IN THE MIDDLE OF THE NIGHT

You've got your team online, and now it's time to lead them through the firestorm. But the key here is **not to panic**—because if you panic, they'll panic. And panic is the last thing you need right now.

Instead, you project calmness. Confidence. The "everything's under control" kind of attitude that you don't necessarily feel, but that your team needs to see. Even if the servers are currently doing their best impression of a dumpster fire, you're going to **steer the ship** through the chaos.

> **"Alright team, we've got this. Let's check the server status and logs. We'll figure it out step by step. No rush—let's just stay focused."**

You're not just **solving a technical problem**; you're guiding your team through it, showing them how to approach a crisis without losing their cool. It's moments like these that build trust, camaraderie, and, let's be honest, future stories they'll tell around the office coffee machine.

THE POWER OF A UNIFIED TEAM

The beauty of a well-assembled team is that each person brings their own strengths. Your DevOps expert is already **deep in the logs**, pulling up data that the rest of the team doesn't even know exists. The backend developer is running queries to check the database, while your front-end developer is making sure nothing visual is broken (even though you all know it's probably not the UI this time).

And the junior dev? Well, they're learning. Watching. Absorbing everything like a sponge. And that's important, too, because they'll be the ones solving these problems in the future.

This is the magic of a crisis situation: it **forces collaboration**. In normal hours, the team might operate in silos, each person focused on their specific domain. But during a crisis? Everyone's working together, tackling the problem from all angles. It's like watching an orchestra come together to play an incredibly stressful symphony.

"Database looks good on my end." "UI checks out here." "Logs show an error with the API connection. We might be onto something."

You watch as the team pieces together the puzzle, and you can't help but feel a sense of pride. This is what leadership is all about—not just solving the problem, but empowering your team to **solve it together**.

The Magic Words: "We've Got It"

After some tense moments of back-and-forth troubleshooting, someone finds the issue. It's a minor glitch in the API configuration—something that wasn't obvious at first glance, but that makes perfect sense once discovered.

"I think I've got it," your backend developer says.

The words every CTO wants to hear in the middle of a crisis. You lean back, a smile tugging at the corners of your mouth.

"Great work! Let's push the fix live and monitor the results. We're almost there, team."

The fix is pushed, and after a few refreshes and anxious seconds, the system starts coming back to life. One by one, the errors disappear, and the site stabilizes. It's a **textbook recovery**, and your team just pulled it off—together.

CELEBRATING THE SMALL WINS

Once the system is back online, you could easily end the call and send everyone back to bed. But you know that **celebrating the win**—no matter how small—is important. It's what keeps morale high and builds a sense of accomplishment.

> **"Fantastic job, everyone. That was a team effort, and we handled it perfectly. Let's document the fix tomorrow, but for now, take a moment to appreciate what we just did. Go get some rest!"**

There's a round of virtual high-fives, maybe even a few GIFs (there's always a well-placed victory GIF in moments like these), and then the team logs off. Crisis averted.

THE OPTIMIST'S TAKEAWAY

Crisis situations aren't just about fixing what's broken. They're about **building trust**, teaching teamwork, and proving to yourself and your team that you can handle whatever the tech gods throw your way.

Calling in the cavalry isn't about giving orders—it's about guiding your team through the storm with a calm, steady hand. It's about empowering them to find the solution and celebrating the win together.

The next time a crisis hits, your team won't panic. They'll know that under your leadership, they can handle anything. Because when the cavalry is assembled and working as one, there's no problem you can't solve.

CHAPTER 4: THE SLACK MELTDOWN

Picture this: The team is gathered (virtually, of course), everyone is ready to tackle the issue head-on, and then, just as you're about to share that critical bit of information, **Slack decides to quit on you**. Because why wouldn't it?

It's one thing when the system goes down, but when the tool you're using to **communicate the fix** goes down? Well, that's a whole new level of disaster.

In this chapter, we explore the joy of trying to manage a crisis while the very tools meant to help you **seemingly conspire against you**.

WHEN COMMUNICATION GOES DARK

It always starts innocently enough. You're typing away in Slack, sharing key findings from the logs (yes, the problem still isn't fully solved), when suddenly, you notice that your message hasn't sent. In fact, it's just sitting there, mocking you with a little spinning icon that says, "Hang tight, we're working on it."

"Slack's down, isn't it?"

You sigh, knowing full well that this is the **icing on the cake**. The system is already down, your team is scrambling, and now your lifeline—the ability to communicate—has flatlined.

There's a moment of silence as everyone in the team chat realizes what's happened. No one wants to believe it, but soon enough, the "connection lost" notifications start rolling in. It's official: **Slack is down.**

You check your internet connection, just to be sure (because it's always worth ruling out the Wi-Fi again). But no, everything else works fine. It's Slack itself that's gone on strike.

THE SCRAMBLE FOR BACKUP COMMUNICATION

Now, this is where leadership really comes in handy. As CTO, you've been through enough of these situations to know that you always need a **backup communication plan**. It's like preparing for a hurricane—you can't rely on just one tool to get you through.

You send out a quick email (yes, **email**—the cockroach of communication tools that never dies), letting the team know that Slack is down and you'll be switching to Plan B.

> **"Alright team, looks like Slack's taking a break. Let's switch to email for now and keep the updates flowing. We'll get through this!"**

The key here is staying calm. You don't let the

team see you sweat, even though internally you're thinking, "Really? Of all the times for this to happen?"

It's just another bump in the road. You've been here before, and you'll be here again. And besides, what's a good crisis without a few extra twists?

THE SEARCH FOR ALTERNATIVES

As the team adjusts to using email (cue the groans, because let's face it, no one likes managing a crisis over email), you start thinking about **long-term solutions**. What happens if Slack goes down in the middle of a major client meeting? What if the communication blackout lasts longer than expected?

You run through the list of backup tools in your mind. Microsoft Teams? Discord? Carrier pigeons? At this point, you're open to anything.

> **"Let's set up a Zoom call. We can hash it out there."**

The team starts migrating to Zoom, and within minutes, you've got everyone back on the same page. Sure, it's not as convenient as Slack, but it works. The team starts sharing updates, troubleshooting the problem, and slowly, you begin to feel like **progress is being made**.

THE REAL CRISIS: USER PERMISSIONS

Just as the team settles into Zoom, a new problem rears its head: **user permissions**. You try to share your screen to walk the team through a potential solution, but Zoom hits you with that dreaded pop-up:

"Host permissions required to share screen."

Host permissions? You are the host! Except... you're not. Apparently, in the rush to get everyone on the call, someone else took the role, and now you're stuck, unable to share your screen while the team waits.

It's a small problem, but in moments like this, even the smallest hurdles feel monumental.

You could get frustrated, but instead, you laugh.

"Looks like Zoom's got a sense of humor tonight. Who's the host? Let's get me set up

so we can keep moving."

The team chuckles, and within moments, the permissions are fixed. You're back in business, screen sharing and all.

THE ENDLESS LOOP OF TWO-FACTOR AUTHENTICATION

Now that you're finally sharing your screen and the team is reviewing potential fixes, someone realizes they need access to an external tool to confirm the issue. But of course, it's protected by **two-factor authentication** (2FA), and the person with access isn't online.

You send a quick text to the team member who has the 2FA token, only to get a reply that reads:

> **"Sorry, I'm not at my desk. I'll send it to you in 10."**

Ten minutes?! In crisis mode, that feels like an eternity. But what can you do? 2FA is one of those necessary evils that ensures security, but also makes you question your life choices when you need access in a hurry.

BACK ON TRACK

Eventually, the team member sends over the 2FA token, access is granted, and the real work can resume. By this point, you've spent more time dealing with communication issues than the actual problem itself. But that's the reality of tech leadership—you're not just solving technical problems; you're solving **people problems**, too.

Once access is restored, the team dives back into the technical details, working through potential fixes. The communication hurdle was just that—a hurdle. Now, with everyone in sync (and on Zoom), progress is finally being made.

CELEBRATING THE WIN (WITH A DASH OF HUMOR)

After what feels like hours of bouncing between different communication platforms, troubleshooting permissions, and waiting for 2FA tokens, the issue is resolved. The system is back online, and the team can finally take a breath.

> **"Great work, everyone. Let's make sure to document this as a 'lesson learned'—never rely on just one communication tool. And maybe keep your 2FA tokens close next time."**

There's a round of laughter as the team logs off, knowing they've just survived yet another disaster. And while the issue itself wasn't the most complicated one you've ever faced, it's the small obstacles—like Slack going down or permission settings—that make these situations memorable.

THE OPTIMIST'S TAKEAWAY

As a leader, part of your job is being **adaptable**. When things go wrong (and they always do), it's your ability to **pivot** that sets the tone for the team. Whether it's switching communication tools, finding new ways to collaborate, or simply rolling with the punches, your calm, optimistic approach keeps the team focused and engaged.

And hey, if you can laugh through it, even better.

Because at the end of the day, technology is never just about the code—it's about the people using it. And when those people come together, even when Slack is down and 2FA is slow, they can accomplish anything.

CHAPTER 5: THE GREAT PASSWORD SEARCH

If there's one thing every tech team dreads more than a system outage, it's the moment when you realize you need access to a critical part of the system and no one can remember the password. It's the tech version of forgetting your keys just as the door slams shut behind you.

We all have **password policies** (or at least we're supposed to), and we all know the importance of keeping things secure. But when it's 3 AM, the system is down, and the only thing standing between you and a solution is a password that's gone AWOL, all that security starts to feel like a cruel joke.

In this chapter, we tackle the infamous **Great Password Search**, the moment when your team scrambles to find that one elusive password that everyone swears someone else has.

THE FALSE CONFIDENCE OF PASSWORD MANAGERS

It all starts with a sense of false confidence. Someone mentions they have the password saved in a **password manager**, which, in theory, is a fantastic idea. But, as with everything in tech, theory and practice often don't align.

"I've got it stored in my password manager. Just give me a second to pull it up."

You wait, hopeful that this will be the fastest crisis resolution in history. But, of course, it's never that simple. A few seconds pass, then a minute, and you realize the person searching for the password is now suspiciously quiet.

"Uh... it's asking me to reset my password manager login. Hold on."

Cue the collective groan. The team knows what's coming next: a **password reset loop** that could take minutes—or longer. And now you're all waiting, like digital detectives in search of the missing key that could unlock your entire system.

PLAN B: CHECK THE SLACK ARCHIVES

When the password manager fails, the next logical step is to **check the Slack archives**. Someone must have posted the password in a private channel at some point, right?

The team dives into Slack, fingers furiously typing away as they search through months (or maybe years) of forgotten messages. And then, the inevitable happens: you find an old message with a password—but it's outdated. Long expired, probably from a time when the system was running Windows 95.

> **"Found one, but it says 'PasswordV2_2019.' I'm guessing that won't work anymore."**

Nope. Definitely not.

It's time to face the reality that **Slack won't save you this time**. You're in deeper than that now. This is going to require some real detective work.

THE PHYSICAL SEARCH: IS IT WRITTEN DOWN SOMEWHERE?

As a CTO, you've trained your team well. You've drilled security practices into them, emphasized the importance of **digital security**, and banned the sticky-note-under-the-keyboard trick. But now, when faced with the possibility that the password is lost in the digital abyss, someone tentatively suggests:

> **"Do you think it's written down somewhere? You know, just in case?"**

You pause for a moment, because while you've made it clear that writing down passwords is a **big no-no**, deep down, you're praying that someone, somewhere, broke that rule just this once. The team scatters, checking desks, flipping through notebooks, and scouring every potential hiding place.

Of course, the hunt comes up empty. No password is scribbled on a sticky note, no "Plan B" security breach in sight. It's time for **Plan C**: pure improvisation.

CONTACTING THE GHOSTS OF TEAMS PAST

When all else fails, there's always the final option: **contacting the person who set up the password in the first place**. The problem? That person hasn't worked for the company in years.

> **"Does anyone have Matt's number? He set this up, like, four years ago."**

There's a brief flurry of activity as the team searches for contact information. Luckily, someone finds Matt's number. You send him a message, crossing your fingers and hoping he still has some relic of that old password stored in the depths of his email archives.

A few minutes later, Matt responds (because of course he's awake at 3 AM, right?). He doesn't have the password, but he does recall something:

> **"I think I set it to something like 'BigProject2020' and then added a bunch**

of random characters. Try that."

It's not much, but it's a start. The team tries every combination they can think of, adding underscores, exclamation marks, numbers —anything to piece together the password.

VICTORY AT LAST: THE PASSWORD EMERGES

And then, after what feels like an eternity of guesswork, someone hits the jackpot. The password works. The system is unlocked, and access is restored.

There's a collective sigh of relief, followed by a few laughs at the absurdity of it all. It took a team effort, a wild guess, and a lot of patience, but the **Great Password Search** is over. And as ridiculous as it was, it's moments like these that remind you that **tech crises aren't always about fixing code—**sometimes, they're about finding the right key to unlock the door.

> "Alright team, great work. Let's get the system up and running, and maybe this time we store that password somewhere a little more... accessible."

You've learned your lesson (again): password management is an art, not a science. And even the best-prepared teams can find themselves on a wild goose chase when that one critical password goes missing.

THE OPTIMIST'S TAKEAWAY

The Great Password Search isn't just about a missing string of characters—it's about how your team comes together to solve a problem, no matter how trivial it may seem. It's a reminder that even the most annoying crises can be resolved with teamwork, patience, and a sense of humor.

At the end of the day, the password isn't just access to the system—it's access to a learning experience. And now your team knows: keep your password manager up to date, and always have a backup plan (just in case).

Because in the world of tech, no crisis is too small to teach a valuable lesson.

CHAPTER 6: WHO PUSHED WHAT TO PRODUCTION?!

You're finally breathing a sigh of relief after hours of troubleshooting. The team's made good progress, and you're certain the worst is behind you. But then, someone casually drops a bombshell:

"Wait, didn't we push an update to production earlier today?"

And just like that, the room (or virtual meeting) goes silent. Everyone's trying to remember who did what, when, and why. It's the tech world's version of **Clue**—except instead of Colonel Mustard with a candlestick, it's Developer Dave with a rogue code commit.

Welcome to the world of **unintended production changes**, where even the smallest update can snowball into a full-blown crisis. In this chapter, we dive into the rollercoaster that is production updates—and the importance of **knowing who pushed what and when**.

THE DAY WAS GOING SO WELL...

It's usually the most peaceful days when these things happen. The system's running smoothly, no major issues, and everyone's happily coding away. You're probably thinking about your next project, confident that today's going to be **uneventful**.

That's when someone on the team remembers an earlier conversation:

> **"We made a small code push to production this morning. Just a minor tweak— nothing serious."**

Famous last words.

Because the thing is, **"nothing serious"** in the tech world has a way of spiraling out of control faster than you can say "rollback." And when no one remembers who pushed the code or what exactly was changed, that's when the real fun begins.

THE CLASSIC FINGER-POINTING FREE ZONE

Now, as a **CTO**, your job in this moment is not to point fingers. In fact, finger-pointing is strictly off-limits. Instead, you take a deep breath and calmly say:

> **"Alright, let's figure this out together. No panic—we just need to track down the change and see what happened."**

You can feel the team shifting into **detective mode**, pulling up GitHub logs, reviewing commit messages, and trying to retrace their steps. This is where everyone suddenly realizes that **naming your commits properly** is important, but naturally, you're faced with the usual suspects:

"Fixed stuff"
"Small update"
"Testing something"
"Oops"

Perfect. Absolutely perfect.

THE GREAT CODE HUNT

The next few minutes (or hours, depending on your luck) are spent combing through the codebase, trying to identify what was pushed and whether it could be responsible for the outage or bug. You're juggling a dozen possibilities—was it the API change? Did someone tweak the server configuration? Is this all the result of that tiny CSS adjustment?

It's like trying to find a needle in a haystack, except the needle might not exist, and you're not even sure if you're looking in the right haystack.

"Found it! There was a small update to the user login system. Shouldn't have caused any issues, though."

The team collectively groans. Because in the tech world, the words **"shouldn't have caused any issues"** are the equivalent of summoning a new crisis.

THE PERILS OF THE SMALL CHANGE

The beauty (and terror) of software development is that **small changes** can have **big consequences**. That minor tweak to the user login system? It turns out it introduced a sneaky bug that only shows up under specific circumstances—circumstances like, say, a system under heavy load at 2 AM.

It's not anyone's fault, really. Changes happen all the time, and no one can predict every possible outcome. But the real challenge is figuring out how to fix it without breaking something else.

> **"Alright, so we've identified the change. Now we just need to roll it back or patch it."**

Simple, right?

ROLLBACK ROULETTE

Rolling back a production update seems easy in theory. Just undo the change, right? But as any seasoned tech leader knows, **rollback roulette** is real. Sure, you might undo the problem, but what if that rollback undoes something else that was actually working? What if it introduces **new issues** that weren't even on your radar?

The team starts discussing options. One group wants to roll back, another suggests a quick patch. The junior dev is suggesting a full system reboot (they're still learning). But no one is rushing in, which is a good sign. They've been trained well— **measure twice, cut once**.

> **"Let's do this smartly. We'll try a patch first, and if that doesn't work, we can consider the rollback."**

You guide the team through the decision-making process, encouraging them to think critically and **weigh the risks**. After all, tech leadership is about teaching the team to make the best decision with the information available—especially when under pressure.

PATCHING THINGS UP

The team gets to work on the patch. It's a straightforward fix, but they're **double-checking everything** this time. Code reviews are happening in real-time, and everyone's taking extra care to ensure this won't cause another ripple effect.

"Patch is ready. Let's deploy and monitor."

With a few keystrokes, the patch is pushed live. You hold your breath for a moment (because no matter how confident you are, there's always that tiny bit of tension), and then... nothing breaks.

Success.

The system stabilizes, and the bug that was causing all the trouble is squashed. The team lets out a collective sigh of relief, and you finally allow yourself to relax, knowing that another crisis has been averted.

LEARNING FROM THE CHAOS

As with every crisis, there are **lessons to be learned**. This time, the lesson is clear: even the smallest change can have a big impact, and keeping track of who pushed what is crucial.

You gather the team for a quick debrief:

> **"Great job, everyone. We handled that like pros. Let's just make sure we document the process so that next time we have a clearer trail."**

The team agrees, and someone suggests maybe, just maybe, they'll start labeling their commits with something more descriptive than **"Oops"**.

THE OPTIMIST'S TAKEAWAY

The real win here isn't just fixing the problem —it's the way the team came together to **solve it collaboratively**. It's about teaching the importance of tracking changes, testing thoroughly, and understanding that **every small decision matters** in a system as complex as ours.

And while mistakes happen (they always will), it's how you **respond** to them that defines your team. No panic, no blame—just a calm, measured approach to problem-solving, one code commit at a time.

Next time a production push goes sideways, you won't sweat it. You've been here before, and you'll be here again. And with a team like yours, there's no challenge you can't handle.

Because in the world of tech, it's not just about what gets pushed to production—it's about **how you handle what happens next**.

CHAPTER 7: THE STRESS FUELED BY CAFFEINE (AND PANIC)

When it comes to solving tech crises, there's one constant that unites every team in the world: **caffeine**. Whether it's coffee, energy drinks, or a combination of both, caffeine is the unsung hero of late-night problem-solving. Of course, there's also panic—good old-fashioned tech panic that sets in around hour three of a problem, when solutions feel elusive and the clock won't stop ticking.

In this chapter, we dive into the **caffeine-fueled frenzy** that every tech team experiences when it feels like they're running on fumes and adrenaline, and how, in those moments, your leadership can turn chaos into clarity.

THE FIRST HOUR: OPTIMISM AND COFFEE

The crisis starts innocently enough. There's a problem (as there always is), but you're confident. It's still early, and the team has only just gathered. Everyone is bright-eyed and optimistic, still running on the energy of their last meal. Someone cracks a joke about how **"this won't take long,"** and the group laughs.

You grab your first cup of coffee, the **fuel of champions**, and take a sip as you start brainstorming solutions with the team. There's a sense of calm in the room—or virtual room, if you're all remote. The system might be down, but there's a **vibe of teamwork** and trust that's keeping everyone focused.

In this first hour, coffee is just coffee. It's your go-to beverage, not a lifeline. But things are about to change.

HOUR TWO: THE SLOW DESCENT

As hour two rolls around, the problem is proving trickier than you thought. You've run through the usual suspects, checked the logs, and tried a few quick fixes. Nothing's working. The calm from the first hour starts to fade, replaced by a slight undercurrent of urgency. You can feel it in the team—things are about to get serious.

"Let's grab another cup of coffee and regroup," you say, more to yourself than anyone else.

Coffee round two: the stakes are higher, the team is starting to feel the pressure, and caffeine is slowly becoming more than just a drink. It's now a **coping mechanism**.

You take a deep breath and guide the team through the next round of troubleshooting. This is where you remind everyone to **stay calm**. After all, you're the leader, and if you start losing your cool, the rest of the team will follow. Coffee is good, but **composure** is better.

HOUR THREE: CAFFEINE IS NOW LIFE

By hour three, you've entered a new realm. The team is starting to feel the stress, and it's clear that the crisis isn't going away anytime soon. Coffee cups are being refilled at an alarming rate, and you can tell that the **caffeine-fueled panic** is creeping in.

> **"I think I've got something,"** one of your devs says, typing furiously.

Everyone gathers around (virtually or physically) to see what they've found. But after a few tense moments, the solution doesn't pan out.

> **"Okay, back to square one,"** you say, trying to keep the tone light.

Inside, you're feeling the **adrenaline**, but on the outside, you're staying steady. You're the glue that's holding the team together, and right now, the only thing stronger than your leadership is the coffee that's coursing through your veins.

At this point, the team is feeling it, too. You've moved from **casual coffee sips** to **emergency coffee chugs**. The room smells like a Starbucks on steroids, and you swear you can hear the faint buzz of energy drinks being cracked open in the background.

HOUR FOUR: THE TURNING POINT

Hour four is when things start to shift. Not necessarily in the direction you'd hoped, but shift they do. The caffeine is **really kicking in now**, and so is the stress. The team is bouncing between ideas, testing one theory after another, and every five minutes someone says:

> **"Wait, I think I've got it!"**

But no one's got it. Not yet, anyway. The caffeine is doing its job, but so is the panic. You know this phase well—it's the moment when **too much energy and too few answers** collide.

As the leader, you know what you need to do: **redirect the team's focus**. You gather everyone back into the conversation and say:

> **"Alright, let's take a step back. What have we learned so far? What's working, and what's not? Let's focus on what we know."**

The team takes a collective breath. You're bringing them back from the brink, helping them refocus on the task at hand. In moments like these, it's not about caffeine or panic—it's about **clarity**. And as the CTO, it's your job to help them find it.

HOUR FIVE: FINDING THE BREAKTHROUGH

By hour five, the coffee cups are empty, and the team is running on pure adrenaline. But something happens. Someone spots a **tiny detail** they missed earlier—a configuration error, a misplaced line of code, something that was easy to overlook but is now glaringly obvious in the aftermath of too much caffeine and not enough sleep.

"I think I've found it," they say, cautiously optimistic.

This time, though, it feels different. The team zeroes in on the detail, checking and rechecking to make sure it's the real issue. And it is.

"That's it. That's the problem."

The room erupts in a wave of tired, caffeine-fueled celebration. The issue has been identified, and the team moves quickly to implement the fix. Within minutes, the system is back online, and just like that, the crisis is over.

THE CALM AFTER THE STORM

Once the fix is in place and the system is stable, the team slowly winds down. You can see the relief on their faces, hear it in their voices. The **panic is gone**, replaced by the satisfaction of knowing they've solved the problem together.

As for you? You've been through enough of these late-night, caffeine-fueled marathons to know that the work doesn't end when the system is back up. Now it's time for the **debrief**, the documentation, and the lessons learned.

But first, you gather the team for a quick message:

> **"Fantastic job, everyone. Let's get some rest and regroup tomorrow. We'll go over everything and make sure we're even more prepared next time. You all handled this perfectly. And maybe tomorrow we can switch to decaf."**

There's a round of tired laughter, and the team starts to log off. You know they'll sleep well

tonight, knowing they conquered another crisis—
and maybe learned a thing or two about caffeine
management in the process.

THE OPTIMIST'S TAKEAWAY

Caffeine is a tech team's best friend and worst enemy. It keeps the team going when energy is low, but it can also **fuel unnecessary panic** if not managed well. As the leader, it's your job to harness that energy, keep the team focused, and guide them through the crisis with calm and clarity.

No matter how many cups of coffee are consumed, or how intense the stress gets, you know that every crisis is an opportunity for the team to grow. And next time, maybe you'll be able to solve it with **just one cup of coffee**—but let's be real, probably not.

Because in the world of tech, the real lesson isn't just about managing the systems—it's about managing the people, the caffeine, and the panic that comes with every late-night crisis.

CHAPTER 8: THE PHANTOM BUG THAT DISAPPEARS

There are few things more frustrating (and strangely amusing) in tech than the **phantom bug** —the one that shows up, wreaks havoc, and then vanishes without a trace. It's the digital equivalent of a ghost story. You know it was real, your team saw it, but now that you're ready to fix it, it's gone. No logs, no error messages, no smoking gun. Just **silence**.

In this chapter, we explore the frustrating yet oddly fascinating world of the phantom bug, where you're left questioning everything— including your own sanity.

THE FIRST
SIGHTING

It always begins the same way: a bug report comes in from a user. Maybe it's a crash on the homepage, maybe it's a button that isn't working, or maybe an entire section of the website has vanished into the digital ether. The user describes it clearly, and you're confident that you can track it down.

> **"I'm sure it's something simple,"** you say to the team, optimism still intact.

But as you pull up the site and navigate to the section in question, everything looks... perfect. The homepage loads fine, the button works, and the missing section is very much present. You scratch your head, wondering if the user sent in the wrong information.

> **"I'm not seeing the issue on my end. Maybe it was a temporary glitch,"** you suggest.

The team nods in agreement, relieved that it's nothing serious. For now.

THE SECOND SIGHTING

Later that day, another report comes in. This time, from a different user, but describing the exact same bug. You're starting to get suspicious. Maybe this phantom bug is more real than you thought.

"Alright, let's dig a little deeper," you say, rolling up your sleeves.

The team starts investigating. You check the logs—nothing. You check the server status—everything's normal. You ask the users to send screenshots, but by the time they do, the bug has disappeared from their screens too.

It's like chasing a shadow. The bug appears, causes chaos, and then **vanishes into thin air**, leaving no trace of its existence.

"Okay, this is officially weird," one of your developers says, echoing everyone's thoughts.

THE GREAT BUG HUNT

Determined to get to the bottom of it, the team dives into **bug hunting mode**. This is where the real detective work begins. You comb through lines of code, check for any recent changes that might have triggered the bug, and even run tests in different environments to try to **recreate the issue**.

Hours pass, and you find nothing. Not a single lead.

"This bug is like Bigfoot—everyone claims to see it, but there's no proof," someone jokes, and the team laughs nervously.

At this point, you're starting to wonder if the bug was even real in the first place. Maybe it was just a glitch, a one-off anomaly that resolved itself. But deep down, you know better. Phantom bugs don't just go away—they **lurk**.

THE FALSE ALARM

Just when you're ready to call it quits, someone on the team thinks they've found the issue. There's a piece of outdated code that could be causing the problem. It's a long shot, but you're willing to try anything at this point.

"Let's patch it and see if that fixes things," you say, cautiously optimistic.

The patch is deployed, and the team waits. For a moment, there's silence. Maybe, just maybe, you've squashed the phantom bug for good.

But then the reports start coming in again. The bug has reappeared, as elusive as ever. You sit back in your chair, realizing that this might be one of those bugs that **refuses to be tamed**.

THE EXISTENTIAL CRISIS

At this point, you and the team are starting to question everything. Is this a real bug? Or is it a product of over-caffeinated minds? Has the bug always been there, lurking in the code, waiting for the right moment to strike?

The longer you chase the phantom bug, the more surreal it feels. You begin to wonder if it's a sign—maybe the universe is telling you to stop overanalyzing everything and just let it be. But that's not how you operate. You can't just leave a bug unsolved, no matter how mysterious it is.

"We'll find it. We just need to keep digging," you tell the team, rallying them for one final push.

THE UNEXPECTED SOLUTION

Just when you're about to give up, the solution reveals itself in the most unexpected way. One of the developers notices a **tiny detail** buried deep in the logs—a timing issue with a third-party service that's causing intermittent errors. It's not your system at all, but an external service that only goes down under specific conditions.

> **"Well, that explains why we couldn't recreate it,"** you say, feeling both relieved and slightly annoyed at how long it took to find.

The fix is simple: adjust the integration with the third-party service to account for the timing issue. You make the change, and sure enough, the bug is gone for good. The phantom bug has been captured.

THE AFTERMATH

Once the bug is squashed, the team feels a mix of **satisfaction** and **exhaustion**. The phantom bug that haunted them for days is finally gone, but the toll it took on their sanity is real. Still, there's a sense of accomplishment in knowing they didn't give up, even when the solution seemed impossible to find.

You send a quick message to the team:

> **"Great work, everyone. The phantom bug has been vanquished. Time to rest and prepare for the next one!"**

There's laughter in the replies. They know another bug will inevitably appear, but for now, they can enjoy the victory.

THE OPTIMIST'S TAKEAWAY

Phantom bugs are a reminder that not everything in tech can be easily explained or solved. Sometimes, the issue isn't in your code at all— it's somewhere out of your control, hiding in the cracks between systems. But that's what makes these challenges so rewarding.

As a leader, your role is to keep the team focused, even when the problem seems unsolvable. **Patience and perseverance** are key, and sometimes, the solution comes from the most unexpected places.

Because in the world of tech, even when the bugs disappear, the lessons you learn from chasing them stick around forever.

CHAPTER 9: THE FIX THAT BREAKS EVERYTHING ELSE

If you've worked in tech long enough, you've experienced the **joy** (or horror) of fixing one problem only to have that fix break something else. It's the domino effect of the tech world—one small change, one little tweak, and suddenly you're dealing with a whole new set of problems. It's as if the system is saying, **"Oh, you thought you solved that? How about I throw you a curveball just to keep things interesting?"**

In this chapter, we dive into the bittersweet world of fixes that create new problems, and how your team can handle it with humor, grace, and maybe a few deep sighs.

THE FIX THAT SHOULD HAVE WORKED

The crisis started small—a minor bug in the notification system. Users were getting delayed notifications, nothing major, just a slight inconvenience. You and your team traced the problem back to a simple code issue, and after a brief discussion, you applied a quick fix. Everything looked good.

"Great job, team. The notifications should be back to normal now," you said confidently, already moving on to the next task.

The system had been running smoothly since the update. No errors, no complaints. It was the kind of small victory that makes you think, **"Well, that was easy."** But in the back of your mind, there's always that lingering doubt. Because in tech, you never really know if a fix is going to stay fixed.

THE PLOT TWIST

A few hours later, a new report comes in. This time, users are having trouble **logging in**. You check the logs, expecting it to be unrelated—maybe a temporary server hiccup or something. But as more reports roll in, you start to get that sinking feeling.

You turn to your team, trying to maintain the positive vibes.

> **"Okay, what's going on with the login system? Let's take a look."**

One of the developers speaks up.

> **"It could be related to the fix we pushed earlier. I mean, the two systems are linked. Maybe the changes to notifications affected the login process?"**

Cue the collective groan.

THE RIPPLE EFFECT

You dive back into the code, tracing the **ripple effect** of the initial fix. As it turns out, the adjustment made to the notification system inadvertently changed how the login system handles user sessions. It wasn't something anyone could have predicted, but there it was—a **domino effect** that started with a seemingly harmless tweak.

> **"Well, this is a new one,"** you say, shaking your head in disbelief.

This is the reality of tech—**every system is interconnected** in ways that sometimes only become clear when things go wrong. Fixing one problem can easily knock something else out of place, and before you know it, you're dealing with a whole new issue.

THE FIX-FOR-THE-FIX DANCE

Now you're in it. The team splits into groups—one group working on **maintaining the notification fix**, while the other works on resolving the **login issue** that the fix caused. It's like a game of whack-a-mole, except the moles are critical system features, and you're desperately trying to keep everything from falling apart.

> **"Let's focus on getting the login system back up first. We'll deal with notifications afterward,"** you say, guiding the team through the chaos.

This is where **prioritization** becomes key. As tempting as it is to try to fix everything at once, you know that focusing on the most immediate problem will save time in the long run. The team agrees, and the work begins.

MORE FIXES, MORE PROBLEMS

Just when you think you've got the login issue under control, someone on the team notices another problem—**users aren't receiving password reset emails**. Apparently, while fixing the login system, something else got knocked loose in the email configuration.

At this point, the team can't help but laugh. It's one of those moments where everything is going wrong, but you've been through enough of these scenarios to know that **staying positive** is the only way through.

> **"Alright, who had 'password reset emails' on their bingo card?"** someone jokes.

Laughter ripples through the team, and just like that, the mood lightens. Yes, the system is having a meltdown, but you've handled worse. This is just another **puzzle** to solve.

ROLLING WITH THE PUNCHES

You quickly realize that fixing one problem at a time isn't going to cut it. The team needs to multitask—fixing the login issue while also restoring the email system. It's not ideal, but you trust your team to **manage both challenges simultaneously**.

> **"Let's take it one step at a time, but tackle both issues together. We've got this."**

This is where the importance of **delegation** comes in. You assign each team member specific tasks, making sure no one is overwhelmed. The key to handling a cascade of problems is to keep the team **focused and organized**. If everyone knows their role, the chaos feels manageable.

And despite the setbacks, the team is in good spirits. Sure, it's frustrating, but they know that these kinds of challenges are just part of the job. And in a strange way, there's something **fun** about it—**solving problems together**, even when it feels like everything's breaking at once.

VICTORY (FOR NOW)

After what feels like an eternity of chasing down problems, the login system is restored. The email system is back up, and notifications are finally working as expected. The team lets out a collective sigh of relief, knowing that they've conquered the latest round of crises.

"Okay, team. Let's make sure everything's stable and then we can call it a night."

As the dust settles, you can't help but feel proud of how the team handled the situation. Sure, it was stressful, but no one panicked, and everyone worked together to find the solution. That's the mark of a **strong team**—being able to stay calm under pressure, even when the fixes seem to be breaking more things than they're solving.

THE DEBRIEF: LESSONS LEARNED

Once the system is back to normal, you gather the team for a quick debrief.

> **"Great work today, everyone. We learned a valuable lesson—always be mindful of how changes in one system can affect others. Let's document everything so we don't run into this again."**

The team agrees, and there's a sense of accomplishment in the air. They've been through the fire, and they came out stronger for it.

And while the fix-for-the-fix dance is never fun, it's a reminder that **no system exists in a vacuum**. Every change has the potential to ripple across the entire platform, and it's up to you and your team to catch those ripples before they turn into waves.

THE OPTIMIST'S TAKEAWAY

Fixing one problem only to cause another is just part of the **tech journey**. It's not a failure—it's a **learning opportunity**. Each time you encounter a ripple effect, your team becomes more prepared for the next one.

As a leader, your job is to guide the team through the chaos, keep spirits high, and remind them that **every problem has a solution**, even if it leads to new problems along the way.

Because in the world of tech, the real challenge isn't just fixing the bug in front of you—it's **anticipating the domino effect** and being ready to handle whatever comes next.

CHAPTER 10: THE CLIENT CELEBRATION, CTO'S INTERNAL SCREAMS

Ah, the post-crisis moment of glory—the one where your client is absolutely **over the moon** about how quickly everything got fixed. They're celebrating, sending congratulatory emails, and maybe even proposing a virtual toast. But behind the scenes, as the CTO, your brain is still **processing the trauma** of what just happened, and you're thinking, **"We're one step away from another disaster."**

In this chapter, we dive into the reality of that post-crisis euphoria, where clients celebrate your success while you quietly brace yourself for the next potential catastrophe.

THE CLIENT'S PERSPECTIVE: A JOB WELL DONE

It usually starts with an enthusiastic email from the client or CEO, filled with phrases like:

"Incredible job!"
"You and your team saved the day!"
"This is why we trust you guys!"

You smile as you read it, because from the client's perspective, everything went perfectly. The system is back up, the bugs are squashed, and the world is a happy place again. They're already thinking about the next big project, excited to move forward now that the crisis is behind them.

"We couldn't be happier with the results," they say, and you can practically hear the virtual applause.

You should be feeling great. After all, you led the team through the fire and came out on top. But instead, a part of you can't shake that nagging feeling that **this crisis was just the beginning**.

THE CTO'S PERSPECTIVE: WHAT'S NEXT?

While the client is celebrating, you're still sitting there thinking about all the **near-misses** that happened during the crisis. Sure, the system is stable now, but you know how fragile everything really is. You're acutely aware that the solution you deployed is more of a **Band-Aid** than a permanent fix, and if one tiny thing goes wrong, you could be right back where you started.

You glance over at your team, who's still running checks and monitoring logs, making sure everything is truly fixed. They're exhausted but relieved, and you can see it in their faces—they're hoping this is the end of today's chaos. But you're already planning for **round two**, because in your experience, the calm never lasts.

THE HIDDEN WORRIES

As CTO, you've learned to wear a mask of calm confidence. It's your job to project stability, even when you're **silently stressing** about what might happen next. While the client is basking in the success, you're quietly making a mental checklist of everything that still needs to be addressed.

> **"Did we check the backup system after the last update?"**
> **"Are the security patches fully up to date?"**
> **"What if another API fails during peak hours?"**

These are the questions that swirl around in your mind as you smile and reply to the client's email with something upbeat, like:

> **"Glad we could help! The team did a fantastic job, and we're happy to have everything running smoothly again."**

But inside, you're already preparing for the next late-night firefight.

THE TEAM'S MOMENT OF GLORY

While you're busy worrying, your team is enjoying their well-earned praise. And rightly so—they've worked hard, tackled the issues head-on, and managed to restore everything to working order. The client's celebration email brings a sense of validation. They're the heroes of the hour, and the victory lap feels good.

You're proud of them. In fact, you're more than proud—you're genuinely grateful for their effort. But while they're ready to enjoy this win and move on, you're the one keeping **both eyes on the horizon**.

> **"Great work, team,"** you say, giving them a much-deserved pat on the back. **"Let's keep monitoring things for a bit longer, just to be safe."**

Because in tech, **safety** means keeping one foot in

crisis mode at all times.

THE UNSEEN THREATS

There's always something **lurking beneath the surface** after a crisis. Maybe it's a new bug waiting to be discovered, or an overlooked configuration that could cause trouble in the future. You know this, but you also know the client doesn't need to hear about it. They want reassurance that everything is fine, and for now, that's exactly what you'll give them.

> **"We'll keep a close eye on things and let you know if any issues pop up,"** you assure them.

Translation: **"We're pretty sure things are stable, but we'll be sleeping with one eye open just in case."**

It's not that you're pessimistic—it's just that you've learned that **nothing stays fixed forever**. And while the client is popping virtual champagne, you're drafting a list of **contingency plans** for when (not if) the next problem arises.

BALANCING CONFIDENCE AND CAUTION

One of the hardest parts of being a CTO is balancing the **public face of confidence** with the **internal reality of caution**. Your job is to keep the client happy, to make them feel secure, and to show them that your team is capable of handling whatever comes their way. But at the same time, you're constantly thinking about **what could go wrong next**.

> **"Everything looks good for now,"** you tell the team, **"but let's be proactive. Check the logs, run some tests, and make sure we're covered on all fronts."**

Your optimism as a leader isn't about pretending everything is perfect—it's about preparing for every possible outcome and making sure your team is ready for whatever happens next.

THE QUIET REFLECTION

Later that evening, after the celebration has died down and the team has logged off, you sit back and take a moment to reflect. Yes, the crisis was resolved, and yes, the client is thrilled, but you know this isn't the end. There will be more bugs, more crashes, more late-night calls. That's just the nature of the job.

And while part of you wishes things could stay calm, another part of you thrives on the **chaos**. After all, it's in these moments of crisis that you see the true strength of your team. It's where you grow as a leader and where the biggest breakthroughs happen.

So you take a deep breath, knowing that tomorrow may bring a new challenge, but tonight, you'll allow yourself a moment of peace.

THE OPTIMIST'S TAKEAWAY

Being a CTO means balancing **celebration and caution**. While your clients may celebrate the wins and assume everything is perfect, your job is to stay **vigilant**—to anticipate the next problem and be ready for it before it happens.

But that doesn't mean you can't enjoy the victories along the way. Every crisis is an opportunity for growth, both for you and your team. And even though the job never really ends, the satisfaction of knowing you've **handled things with grace and optimism** is its own reward.

Because in the world of tech, every crisis is just another chance to show what your team is capable of—and to remind yourself why you love what you do, even when everything is on fire.

CHAPTER 11: THE TEAM FINALLY SLEEPS...UNTIL THE NEXT CALL

After every crisis comes the moment of relief. The bugs are squashed, the system is stable, and your team has finally logged off for the night. Everyone can breathe, celebrate, and most importantly, **get some much-needed sleep.** But, as any seasoned tech professional knows, the peace is always **temporary.** It's not a matter of if the next crisis will strike, but **when.**

In this chapter, we dive into the moment when your team finally relaxes, only to be woken up by **another late-night call**—because in tech, **sleep is a luxury.**

THE POST-CRISIS COMA

After a long night of firefighting, the team has earned their rest. Everyone's been through the wringer, but there's a sense of accomplishment as they log off. The system is working perfectly (for now), and there's nothing left to do except **collapse into bed**.

You send out one final message to the team:

> **"Great work, everyone. Get some sleep. You've earned it."**

There's a round of tired but satisfied replies. The team is spent, and you can practically hear them logging off, one by one, as they head for the nearest pillow. You smile, feeling proud of how they handled the chaos. You even allow yourself to imagine a **calm, crisis-free night**.

THE FALSE SENSE OF SECURITY

The first hour after a crisis is **deceptively peaceful**. You check the logs, monitor the system, and everything looks stable. No new errors, no unexpected outages. It's almost enough to make you believe that you can close your laptop and enjoy a good night's sleep.

But deep down, you know better. You've been here before, lulled into a false sense of security, only to be jolted awake by the **dreaded late-night call**. Still, hope springs eternal, and you head to bed with the optimistic belief that tonight will be different.

> **"Maybe this time we'll actually get some sleep,"** you mutter to yourself.

THE CALM BEFORE THE STORM

For the first few hours, everything is blissfully quiet. The team is asleep, the system is running smoothly, and the night stretches out before you like a gift. You finally start to unwind, thinking that maybe—just maybe—the worst is behind you.

But then it happens. Your phone buzzes.

It's always a single buzz at first, as if testing the waters, deciding whether or not to fully disturb you. You glance over at it, hoping it's just a random notification, but the screen lights up with a **Slack alert**.

"Urgent: System error detected. Need assistance."

You let out a sigh. Of course. The night was going too smoothly. This is just the universe's way of reminding you that **calm doesn't last**.

THE RALLYING CALL

You fire off a quick message to the team, apologizing in advance for disturbing their rest, but knowing that there's no other option.

"Sorry to wake everyone, but we've got an issue that needs attention."

You brace yourself for the groggy replies, expecting frustration. But instead, the team rallies. One by one, they come online, still half-asleep but ready to tackle the problem.

"No worries. What's the situation?"
"Just got up—let's fix this."
"On my way to the computer."

It's moments like this that make you proud as a leader. Sure, no one wants to be woken up in the middle of the night, but your team understands that this is **part of the job**. They don't complain —they jump into action, ready to solve whatever's thrown at them.

THE SLEEP-DEPRIVED DEBUGGING SESSION

With the team online, the **sleep-deprived troubleshooting** begins. There's something almost comical about these moments—everyone's a little groggy, a little grumpy, but still **incredibly focused**. The energy is different from the earlier crisis. Now it's fueled by **pure adrenaline** and the knowledge that if they fix this quickly, they might still catch a few hours of sleep.

> **"Looks like the issue is with the load balancer,"** one of the developers says, their voice thick with exhaustion.

> **"Let's run a quick check. Shouldn't take long to fix,"** another chimes in, already typing away.

You can tell the team is tired, but they're **still**

sharp. They move quickly, checking the logs, rerouting traffic, and deploying fixes. There's no panic—just a quiet determination to get the job done so everyone can return to bed.

THE MIDNIGHT REALIZATIONS

As you work through the problem, you notice something funny about these late-night sessions. The team, while sleep-deprived, is often more **creative** during these moments. The usual filters are gone, and people start throwing out ideas that might not have come up during the day.

> **"What if we adjust the timeout settings to reduce server strain? It might give us more breathing room."**

> **"I wonder if this issue is related to that patch we applied last week. Could be a long-shot, but it's worth checking."**

It's during these midnight realizations that some of the best ideas are born. There's no overthinking, no second-guessing—just pure **problem-solving mode**. And somehow, despite the exhaustion, the team manages to make progress.

VICTORY IN THE WEARY HOURS

After what feels like an eternity (but is probably only an hour or two), the issue is resolved. The system is stable again, and the team lets out a collective sigh of relief.

"Issue fixed. We're back online," someone reports.

You can feel the exhaustion in the messages, but also the satisfaction. The team has pulled off another **late-night victory**, and now they can finally return to the sleep they so desperately need.

"Great work, everyone. Get some rest— we'll debrief tomorrow."

There's a round of tired acknowledgments before the team logs off, heading back to their beds, knowing full well that this won't be the last late-night call. But for now, they've earned a few more hours of sleep.

THE INEVITABLE REFLECTION

As the team logs off, you stay online a little longer, reflecting on what just happened. This wasn't the first late-night call, and it certainly won't be the last. But that's part of the job. You know that. Your team knows that. And despite the exhaustion, there's a certain **camaraderie** that comes from handling these moments together.

It's in these sleep-deprived sessions that you see the true strength of your team. They don't just handle crises—they **grow** from them. Each challenge makes them more resilient, more capable, and more prepared for whatever comes next.

As you finally shut your laptop and head back to bed, you remind yourself that you're **leading an incredible team**, one that can handle anything—even on two hours of sleep.

THE OPTIMIST'S TAKEAWAY

Late-night calls are part of the **unwritten contract** of working in tech. The system will go down, the bugs will show up, and sleep will often be interrupted. But it's in these moments that your team's true character shines.

As a leader, your job is to keep the team motivated, even when they're exhausted, and remind them that every challenge is an opportunity to grow. And while the crises will keep coming, so will the victories—one sleep-deprived fix at a time.

Because in the world of tech, the team that **rallies together** at 2 AM is the team that can handle anything.

CHAPTER 12:
THE RECURRING
NIGHTMARES
OF THE CTO

There's a funny thing about working in tech: even when everything is going smoothly, your brain can't quite let go of all the past crises. Whether you're out at a family dinner, lying in bed, or taking a shower, somewhere in the back of your mind, you're replaying **"what if" scenarios**—those late-night disasters, the bugs that wouldn't die, or the near-misses that almost took everything down.

In this chapter, we explore the **recurring nightmares** every CTO faces, those moments of imagined (and sometimes real) chaos that play on a loop in your head, long after the systems are back online.

THE PHANTOM ALERT: IT'S PROBABLY FINE... RIGHT?

It always starts innocuously. You're relaxing, maybe even enjoying a rare evening without your laptop in sight, when you feel your phone buzz. It's just one notification—probably a random app update or a low battery warning. But in your CTO brain, every buzz is potentially **a server on fire**.

"It's nothing," you tell yourself, though your heart rate has already spiked.

But the problem is, it's never just nothing. You've been trained by years of crises to expect the worst. The first sign of trouble is usually a small one, like that phantom buzz. And so, despite your better judgment, you check your phone.

"Nope, it's just a reminder to buy groceries. But you never know..."

You can't help it—you double-check Slack, your email, and every monitoring tool just to be sure everything is fine. It's the digital equivalent of checking the locks before bed, except in your world, the locks are **load balancers, databases, and APIs.**

The "What If?" Scenarios

As a CTO, your mind is constantly running through a series of worst-case scenarios, even when everything seems fine. It's not pessimism —it's **preparedness**. After all, you've seen enough things go wrong to know that the next crisis is always just a few missed packets away.

> **"What if the server goes down during peak traffic?"**
> **"What if that patch we applied last week causes an unexpected bug?"**
> **"What if the system is secretly down and we haven't even noticed yet?"**

These thoughts follow you everywhere—during dinner with friends, on your morning run, even when you're trying to fall asleep. It's not that you're paranoid. You've just learned that tech systems are like toddlers—**quiet usually means trouble is brewing.**

THE FLASHBACKS: REMEMBER THAT TIME...?

Every CTO has **war stories**, and sometimes they come back to haunt you. Maybe it's that time the entire system went down for four hours because of a rogue update, or when a small database migration took down half the company's operations for a day.

These memories resurface at the most inconvenient times. You'll be sitting in a meeting, discussing a new feature rollout, and suddenly your brain goes:

> **"Remember that time the database failed during a simple backup process? Yeah, let's not do that again."**

It's like a highlight reel of **everything that could go wrong**, playing on a loop in your mind. The good news? These flashbacks keep you sharp. You're always thinking three steps ahead, making sure that whatever happened in the past doesn't happen again.

The bad news? They sometimes make it hard to enjoy a peaceful weekend.

THE SNEAKY BUGS YOU DIDN'T CATCH

Then there are the bugs you're sure are hiding somewhere in the codebase, just waiting to cause chaos. You can't prove it, but you know they're there, biding their time until **just the right moment** to strike.

"What if there's a bug in that last update? No one's reported it yet, but what if…"

These are the bugs that keep you awake at night— the ones no one's noticed yet, but you know will surface eventually. Maybe it'll be a minor issue, like a misplaced decimal point, or maybe it'll be something bigger, like a data corruption error that brings down the entire system.

You've been through this before: the **phantom bugs** that appear without warning, and the hours spent trying to figure out where they came from. You prepare for them, but there's always that nagging worry that **one day**, the perfect storm will hit, and you'll be left scrambling to patch things up.

The "All Systems Go" Anxiety

Even when all systems are **green**, you can't relax. In fact, the quiet moments are sometimes the most anxiety-inducing. You'll check the dashboards, see everything running smoothly, and instead of feeling relief, you feel... suspicious.

> **"Everything looks fine, but what if the monitoring tools are wrong?"**

It's like when you're driving down an empty highway, and everything is calm, but you keep thinking something must be lurking around the corner. The silence is **too perfect**, and your mind starts running through all the ways things could go wrong, even when nothing seems amiss.

But this is part of the job—learning to live with the constant low-level buzz of anxiety, even when things are working well. It's a strange combination of **paranoia and optimism**, knowing that while you expect things to go wrong, you and your team are fully capable of handling it when they do.

THE UNEXPECTED CALL: NOT AGAIN...

And then there's the nightmare scenario that never fully leaves your mind: the **unexpected call**. You're in the middle of a family gathering or a rare vacation when your phone rings. It's your team or, worse, the CEO.

You answer, already knowing what's coming.

"Hey, we've got a bit of a situation..."

In that moment, you're instantly transported back to crisis mode. It doesn't matter where you are or what you're doing—when the call comes, you spring into action. Suddenly, you're coordinating the team, issuing instructions, and solving problems, all while mentally kissing your evening plans goodbye.

As a CTO, you've accepted that these calls are

just part of life. But that doesn't make them any less stressful when they happen. Every call is a reminder that the systems you're responsible for never truly sleep—**and neither do you**.

TURNING NIGHTMARES INTO STRATEGY

But here's the thing: as annoying as these recurring CTO nightmares are, they serve a purpose. They keep you **sharp**, always thinking ahead and preparing for the worst. In many ways, these "nightmares" are just your brain doing **preventive maintenance**—working through potential issues so you can avoid them in reality.

You've learned to use this constant hum of worry to your advantage. Instead of letting it stress you out, you turn it into **actionable strategy**. You double-check the systems, reinforce your monitoring tools, and make sure your team is always prepared for the unexpected.

Because in the world of tech, the worst-case scenario isn't a nightmare—it's just another challenge waiting to be solved.

THE OPTIMIST'S TAKEAWAY

As a CTO, your brain is always working overtime, anticipating problems and running through worst-case scenarios. But this is exactly what makes you and your team **resilient**. You're not just waiting for the next crisis—you're preparing for it.

Sure, the recurring nightmares of a CTO are real, but they're also a reminder of how much you care about keeping things running smoothly. And every time a crisis hits, you're ready—because you've already worked through the solution in your mind a hundred times before.

So, while the nightmares might never go away, neither does your ability to handle whatever comes your way.

Because in the world of tech, **anticipation** is half the battle.

CHAPTER 13: THE DOCUMENTATIO N BLACK HOLE

If there's one thing every CTO dreads almost as much as a major system failure, it's the realization that no one knows **where the documentation is—** or worse, that it doesn't exist. In the heat of a crisis, good documentation can be your lifeline. Without it, you're left fumbling through **guesswork, tribal knowledge, and frantic Slack messages** to figure out how things are supposed to work.

In this chapter, we delve into the chaos of working without documentation, how it sends everyone scrambling, and how you somehow always manage to find a way forward—even if it means writing the missing documentation **on the fly**.

The Discovery: "Where's the Doc?"

It's the middle of a routine maintenance task— nothing major, just a simple update to an existing system. You're in a meeting, confident that the team can handle it without any issues. Everything seems to be going well... until you get the call.

"Hey, quick question—do you know where the documentation for this process is?"

You pause. The question itself is innocent enough, but you immediately know this means trouble. Because if the team is asking you where the documentation is, that means **no one has it**. The worst-case scenario has already begun.

You log in, mentally bracing yourself, and reply with the question that haunts every tech leader:

"Have you checked the shared folder?"

There's a long silence on the other end. Then:

"Yeah... it's not there."

Of course it's not. **It never is**.

THE DESCENT INTO CHAOS

With the documentation nowhere to be found, you can feel the panic start to creep into the team. What was supposed to be a routine task now has everyone scrambling to figure out how to move forward.

> **"Check the internal wiki. Maybe it's there."**
> **"Has anyone asked the person who wrote the original code?"**
> **"Wait, wasn't there a Confluence page for this at some point?"**

Suddenly, the team is scattered in different directions, searching through Slack archives, email chains, and forgotten folders, trying to piece together how this part of the system is supposed to work.

As the CTO, you watch this unfold with a mix of resignation and amusement. It's not the first time this has happened, and it certainly won't be the last. Every tech company has its **documentation black hole**, and today, your team has just fallen into it.

The "Tribal Knowledge" Phase

With no official documentation in sight, the team moves to the next phase: **relying on tribal knowledge**. This is when you find out who on the team has been around long enough to remember how things were set up three or four years ago— back when the system was first built.

> **"I think I remember how this works,"** one of the senior developers says, but they don't sound entirely sure.

> **"Didn't we change the process two versions ago? Or maybe it was last year...?"** another dev chimes in.

At this point, the conversation becomes a strange mix of half-remembered details and wild guesses. It's like trying to solve a puzzle where half the pieces are missing and the box with the picture has been thrown away.

You jump in with a calm, steady voice.

> **"Alright, let's piece together what we know and take it step by step. We'll figure this out."**

You're leading them through a minefield of forgotten configurations, long-gone processes, and undocumented changes. But you know the team can handle it. They always do.

WRITING DOCUMENTATIO N... ON THE FLY

Since you're already in the middle of the task, you know there's no time to delay. So, what's the solution when documentation is missing? You write it **as you go**.

> **"Let's document everything we're doing while we troubleshoot this,"** you suggest, turning what could have been a frustrating setback into an opportunity for growth.

The team nods in agreement, and suddenly, there's a new sense of focus. While some team members are trying to reverse-engineer the original process, others are creating a real-time playbook, documenting every step they take. It's messy, sure, but it's better than nothing.

> **"Okay, so step one is... we think this configuration file needs to be updated. Let's note that down."**

"Got it. Also, don't forget to add that the database schema was changed in version 2.1—that's probably why the original instructions don't work anymore."

It's not pretty, but it's progress. And as the team documents the steps they're taking, you know you're **building something useful for the future—** even if that future is only a few hours away when the next person asks, "Hey, where's the doc?"

THE UNEXPECTED HELP

Just when it seems like you're getting a handle on the situation, a miracle happens. Someone on the team gets a ping from a former colleague who left the company months ago but, for some reason, still checks Slack now and then.

"Hey, I think I have a copy of the old documentation. Let me send it over."

You can't believe it. A copy of the **original documentation**? It's like finding buried treasure—though, given how outdated the system probably is, you're not entirely sure it'll be useful. But hey, you're desperate.

The file arrives, and as expected, it's a bit of a mess. Half of it is no longer relevant, and the other half references systems that no longer exist. But there's just enough information in there to help guide the team.

"Okay, we can work with this. Let's cross-reference it with what we've figured out so far."

It's not perfect, but it's enough to get the task done. The team pushes through, using the combination of old documentation, tribal knowledge, and on-the-fly notes to get the system back up and running.

THE DOCUMENTATION DECREE

Once the task is complete and everything is working smoothly again, you gather the team for a quick debrief.

> **"Alright, team. Great work getting that done, but we need to talk about documentation. Let's make sure that moving forward, we keep everything up to date and in one place."**

The team groans in unison. They've heard it all before. Everyone knows that documentation is important, but in the fast-paced world of tech, it's often the last thing on anyone's mind.

Still, you're determined. As the CTO, you know that good documentation is the difference between a minor inconvenience and a full-blown crisis. You send out a gentle reminder:

> **"Let's all pitch in to keep the**

documentation clean and accessible. You never know when you'll need it."

The team nods in agreement, though you can already see the inevitable cycle repeating itself. But for now, you've made progress, and that's enough.

THE OPTIMIST'S TAKEAWAY

The **documentation black hole** is real, and every tech team falls into it at some point. But as frustrating as it can be, these moments are also opportunities for growth. They remind you and your team that no system is perfect, and that building strong processes—including proper documentation—takes time.

As a leader, your job is to turn the chaos into **organization**, to guide the team through the fog of missing information and help them build something better for the future. Because while documentation may seem like a small thing, it's the foundation that keeps everything running smoothly when the next crisis hits.

So, yes, the documentation black hole will always exist—but so will your ability to navigate it.

Because in the world of tech, **you can always write the solution**—even if it's after the fact.

CHAPTER 14: THE MEETING THAT COULD HAVE BEEN AN EMAIL

Every CTO knows the **dreaded meeting**—those extended sessions that somehow manage to feel both urgent and utterly pointless. In the fast-paced world of tech, time is money (and sanity), and nothing eats away at productivity like a meeting that drags on for an hour but could have been summed up in a **three-sentence email**.

In this chapter, we explore the chaos of meetings that spiral out of control, how to survive them without losing your mind, and the subtle art of steering the conversation back to **actual solutions**.

THE AGENDA THAT PROMISES TOO MUCH

It always starts with an agenda that seems reasonable enough. You glance at it and think, **"This should be quick."** The items listed are fairly straightforward: updates on projects, a discussion about a new feature, maybe a brief mention of the latest system patch. You tell yourself it's just another routine check-in.

But then the meeting starts, and right away, you can feel it spiraling out of control.

> **"Before we dive into the agenda, I just wanted to bring up this other issue…"**

Uh-oh. You've seen this movie before. What was supposed to be a 30-minute meeting is now veering off into an uncharted territory of **unrelated topics**, side conversations, and debates that feel like they're happening in slow motion. You glance at the clock and silently pray this doesn't turn into an **all-hands crisis intervention**.

THE TANGENTS BEGIN

Meetings have a way of becoming **black holes** for tangents. A conversation about updating the code repository quickly morphs into a philosophical debate about project management workflows. Someone throws out a question that wasn't on the agenda, and suddenly you're knee-deep in a discussion about whether or not to switch task management tools.

You try to stay engaged, but your brain is already flashing red lights.

> **"Is this really the best use of our time?"** you think to yourself.

You smile, nod, and throw in a **diplomatic response** now and then to keep things moving:

> **"That's a good point. Let's table that for now and focus on the task at hand."**

You know the drill—**redirect the conversation** before it derails entirely. But you also know that once the tangents begin, it's like trying to stop a runaway train.

THE INTERRUPTIONS AND OVER-EXPLANATIONS

As the meeting drags on, the interruptions begin. Someone keeps cutting in with "just one more thing," while others over-explain every detail. You love your team, you really do, but there's only so much you can handle before you start mentally rewriting the meeting into an **email draft**.

> **"We could have handled this with a simple email thread,"** you mutter under your breath, glancing at your notes, which now include doodles of servers on fire.

The over-explanations are the worst. The simplest ideas turn into long-winded explanations that feel like tech support manuals. You try to stay patient, but internally, you're already drafting the **summary email** you'll need to send afterward to refocus everyone.

THE BREAKTHROUGH (MAYBE?)

After what feels like a lifetime, someone finally suggests something useful—a **breakthrough** in the conversation that feels like it might actually lead to a solution.

> **"I think if we adjust the load balancing thresholds, it should help with the system performance issue."**

Suddenly, the room (or virtual meeting) shifts. Everyone is now talking about the problem that actually matters. It's the moment you've been waiting for—actual **progress**.

You jump in to solidify the point:

> **"Great suggestion. Let's get that into action and follow up after it's been tested."**

For a brief moment, you think this might be the end of the meeting. The team seems ready to move forward, everyone nods in agreement, and you glance at the clock, hopeful that you've escaped with enough time to actually get some work done.

But no. It's not over yet.

The Final Round of "One Last Thing"

Just as you're about to close the meeting, someone hits you with the infamous **"one last thing"**—the dreaded add-on that extends the conversation by another 15 minutes.

> **"Before we wrap up, I just wanted to discuss the upcoming patch deployment…"**

Here we go again. You know this will spiral into another round of questions and potential delays. You glance at your laptop, seeing your unread Slack messages piling up, and think about all the other things you could be doing. But you stay professional:

> **"Alright, let's touch on that briefly, but we'll need to wrap this up soon so everyone can get back to their work."**

THE ART OF ENDING A MEETING

Ending a meeting that's gone off the rails is like trying to land a plane in a storm—**delicate, but necessary**. You have to do it with just the right amount of firmness and politeness, without making anyone feel rushed or unheard.

You start by summarizing the key points:

> **"Okay, just to recap, we've got the load balancing adjustment as the next step, and we'll monitor the patch deployment separately. I'll send out an email with action items so we're all on the same page."**

This is your escape hatch. By promising to follow up via email, you're signaling that the conversation will continue **offline**, where it belongs. The team nods in agreement, and you can finally close the meeting.

> **"Thanks, everyone. Let's wrap up and get**

back to it."

You hit "Leave Meeting" faster than you'd care to admit, and for the first time in an hour, you feel free.

THE AFTERMATH: THE EMAIL THAT COULD HAVE BEEN

As the meeting ends, you draft the email you wish you could have sent in the first place. It's succinct, to the point, and about 90% shorter than the meeting itself.

> **"Hey team, just a quick update: we'll be adjusting the load balancing thresholds today. Keep an eye on the patch deployment, and let me know if you see any issues. Thanks!"**

There. Done. **Three sentences** that summarize an hour of back-and-forth tangents, over-explanations, and unnecessary detours. You hit "Send" and feel a wave of relief.

But you also know this isn't the last time you'll be in one of these meetings. They're a fact of life in tech, just like bugs and system crashes. All you can do is **survive** them and find ways to keep things productive, even when the conversation goes off course.

THE OPTIMIST'S TAKEAWAY

Meetings that should have been emails are part of the **CTO experience**. They're frustrating, time-consuming, and often filled with unnecessary detours, but they're also a chance to practice **leadership in chaos**. It's your job to steer the conversation, keep the team focused, and make sure you leave with actionable steps.

As much as you might dread these meetings, they're also where some of the best ideas emerge—once you sift through the tangents, of course.

Because in the world of tech, **progress doesn't always happen in a straight line**. Sometimes it takes a meandering conversation and a few extra emails to get there.

CHAPTER 15: THE TEST ENVIRONMENT ISN'T QUITE REALITY

In tech, there's a common phrase that brings both **hope and terror: "It worked in the test environment."** The idea of a perfect test environment is a comforting one—a controlled space where you can tinker with new features, squash bugs, and experiment with wild ideas before rolling them out to the world. But more often than not, the test environment is a **beautiful lie**. It's where everything seems perfect, only to have those same "working" solutions explode the moment they hit **production**.

This chapter dives into the false security of the test environment, why things always go haywire when you deploy them for real, and how you manage the fallout with a smile (and maybe a cup of strong coffee).

THE DREAM: EVERYTHING'S PERFECT IN TEST

It starts with the best of intentions. The team has been working hard on a new feature for weeks. It's been tested, re-tested, and signed off on by **everyone**. In the test environment, it works flawlessly. Smooth as butter. It even handles the edge cases with ease. You've got green lights across the board.

> **"The feature is ready for production,"** someone says confidently, and you nod, feeling like a proud parent.

Everyone's excited. There's a collective sense of accomplishment as the team prepares for the big rollout. The test environment has given everyone a sense of **invincibility**. After all, if it works there, it'll work everywhere, right?

THE COLD REALITY OF PRODUCTION

Ah, if only that were true. The moment the code is pushed to production, everything changes. The perfect, bug-free feature from the test environment suddenly starts throwing errors you've never seen before. Users are reporting glitches that didn't exist a few hours ago. The system feels like it's held together with **duct tape and good intentions**.

"It worked perfectly in test!" someone cries, staring in disbelief at the logs.

Of course it did. The test environment is like a **perfectly calm lake**, where nothing disturbs the surface. But production? That's the **ocean**, where you're facing unexpected waves, sharks, and the occasional tsunami. It's a whole different beast.

The "It Should Work" Stage

Once the initial shock wears off, the team dives into **problem-solving mode**. The logs are pulled up, the error messages are analyzed, and everyone is scratching their heads, wondering how the test environment could have been so misleading.

"This doesn't make sense. It should work."

Ah, yes. The famous "it should work" stage. This is where logic tells you one thing, but reality tells you another. You've run the same scenarios a hundred times in test, but now, under the strain of real users, real data, and real-world unpredictability, the feature is **crumbling**.

At this point, you're stuck between frustration and amusement. You can't help but laugh at the absurdity of it all—how something that worked so perfectly in isolation could fall apart so spectacularly in the real world.

THE UNKNOWN VARIABLES

One of the hardest things about production environments is the sheer number of **unknown variables**. No matter how well you've prepared, there's always something you didn't account for —an unexpected user behavior, a rare data configuration, or a hidden server quirk.

You and your team start piecing together the clues. It's like a tech version of **CSI**, where each log file and error message is a clue that leads you closer to the truth.

> **"I think the issue is with how the API is handling live traffic. We didn't see this in test because the load wasn't as high."**

Of course. The test environment was too **predictable**, too structured. But in production, there's chaos. Users don't always follow the script, and real-world traffic can overwhelm even the most carefully planned systems.

> **"Let's adjust the API settings and push a**

fix."

THE PATCH THAT SAVES THE DAY (FOR NOW)

The team quickly huddles to create a patch. It's not ideal, but it'll hold things together until a more permanent solution can be implemented. The patch is deployed, and the errors start to disappear. The system stabilizes, and the users stop complaining (for now).

"We're back online," someone says, and there's a collective sigh of relief.

You've dodged the bullet this time. But deep down, you know this is only a temporary victory. The test environment has lulled you into a false sense of security before, and it'll do it again. That's just the nature of the beast.

THE POST-MORTEM: WHAT WENT WRONG?

Once the crisis is over, you gather the team for the inevitable post-mortem. What went wrong? Why did the test environment lie to us? And how can we avoid this next time?

> **"The test environment was too controlled,"** someone says. **"It didn't replicate the real-world traffic and variability we see in production."**

That's usually the answer. Test environments, no matter how robust, can't fully mimic the unpredictability of the real world. But there are ways to get closer. You start brainstorming ideas:

> **"We should introduce more realistic traffic simulations in test."**
> **"Maybe we can use real-world data sets to test edge cases."**
> **"Let's make sure the load testing actually**

pushes the limits of what the system can handle."

It's all good advice, and you take note of it for next time. You know you can't make the test environment perfect, but you can make it **better**.

THE OPTIMIST'S TAKEAWAY

As frustrating as it is when the test environment betrays you, it's a reminder that tech is never as simple as it seems in a controlled setting. The real world is messy, unpredictable, and full of surprises. And while test environments are a good start, they're only part of the equation.

The key is to **expect the unexpected**, to prepare for things to go wrong, and to have a team that can quickly adapt when they do. As a CTO, you're not just managing technology—you're managing the **chaos that comes with it**.

So the next time your perfect test environment turns into a production nightmare, don't sweat it. You've been here before, and you'll be here again. And each time, you'll learn a little more about how to make the system stronger.

Because in the world of tech, **nothing is ever as simple as it seems**—and that's half the fun.

CHAPTER 16:
THE LONG-LOST
CODEBASE

Every tech team has its mysteries—those pieces of code that no one remembers writing, but that are somehow critical to the entire system's functionality. These relics of the past live deep in the codebase, untouched for years, quietly doing their job… until something goes wrong. And then, like an ancient curse, that forgotten code comes back to haunt you.

In this chapter, we explore the **forgotten codebase conundrum**, where no one knows who wrote it, no one knows why it exists, and yet, everyone knows that messing with it could be disastrous.

THE FIRST SIGN
OF TROUBLE

It always begins innocently. A new team member, fresh and enthusiastic, suggests updating an old feature. They open up the codebase, look at the files, and ask a simple question:

"What does this file do?"

The moment you hear that, your stomach sinks. You know that file. It's been in the codebase since the dawn of time. No one's touched it, no one knows exactly what it does, but it's **too risky to delete**.

"Oh, that? Yeah... we don't mess with that," you say, trying to suppress the memories of past attempts to clean it up.

But the damage is done. Curiosity has been sparked, and now the team is diving into the forgotten corners of the codebase, stirring up old ghosts that were better left undisturbed.

THE MYSTERY DEEPENS

The team gathers around the code like archaeologists examining an ancient artifact. There are variables that don't make sense, functions that seem unrelated to anything, and comments that are either cryptic or completely missing.

"Has anyone touched this in the last five years?"

"I'm pretty sure this predates our version control."

"Wait, did we inherit this from a previous team? Or maybe it's from a legacy system?"

No one knows. The original author is long gone, having either moved on to another company or ascended to CTO somewhere else, leaving behind this code as a reminder of their presence.

The team debates for a while, trying to piece together the purpose of the code. It's like trying to solve a riddle with half the clues missing, and the answers hidden behind a wall of legacy code.

THE FEAR OF CHANGE

Eventually, someone asks the inevitable question:

"Should we refactor it? Or just delete it?"

And that's when the real fear sets in. Because while no one knows exactly what the code does, they do know one thing for sure: **messing with it could bring down the entire system**.

"I don't know... it's been stable for years. Do we really want to take that risk?"

There's a nervous silence. Everyone knows that touching the code could unleash **chaos**—a domino effect of bugs and crashes that would send the team into a tailspin for weeks.

"Let's leave it for now. If it's not broken, there's no need to fix it," you say, using the classic line of every CTO who has stared into the abyss of legacy code and decided to walk away.

The "We'll Deal With It Later" Strategy

Once the decision is made to leave the code untouched, there's a collective sigh of relief. The mystery remains unsolved, but for now, that's a good thing. The risk of waking the sleeping giant has been avoided.

"We'll document it and deal with it later," you say, knowing full well that "later" means "never."

And so, the code is labeled with a warning, a vague comment that essentially reads, **"Do not touch unless absolutely necessary."** It becomes the **code equivalent of a cursed object**, sitting quietly in the repository, waiting for the next brave (or foolish) developer to come along and ask the same question:

"What does this file do?"

THE RISKS OF LEGACY CODE

This is the reality of tech. Every system, no matter how modern, has some form of **legacy code** lurking in its depths. It's code that was written for a reason—once. But over time, as systems evolve and teams change, that reason gets lost. All that remains is a ticking time bomb, waiting for the moment when someone makes a change that brings everything crashing down.

As CTO, you've learned to respect these relics. You don't have to like them, but you do have to acknowledge that they hold the system together in ways you might never fully understand.

THE TEMPTATION TO REWRITE EVERYTHING

There's always that part of you that wants to take a sledgehammer to the entire thing and start over. The temptation to rewrite everything from scratch is strong. After all, how hard could it be to rebuild the system with modern tools, clean code, and proper documentation?

But then reality sets in. You remember all the times you've tried to fix one small thing, only to discover that it was connected to **three other things** that were connected to **ten more things**. And before you know it, you're in over your head, trying to solve problems that never existed before you started.

> **"Let's not try to fix what isn't broken,"** you remind yourself.

It's a tough decision, but it's the right one. Sometimes, the best course of action is to leave the legacy code where it is, and focus on the things you **can** improve.

THE OPTIMIST'S TAKEAWAY

The long-lost codebase isn't just a relic of the past—it's a reminder of the evolution of your system, your team, and your company. It's the embodiment of **every decision, patch, and workaround** that got you to where you are today.

And while the temptation to clean it up, refactor it, or delete it entirely is strong, there's value in knowing when to let it be. The key is **balance**—knowing which parts of the system need attention and which parts are best left untouched (for now).

Because in the world of tech, **some mysteries are better left unsolved**. And if the system is stable, sometimes the smartest thing you can do is tip your hat to the unknown developers who came before you, and move on to the next challenge.

CHAPTER 17: THE FEATURE CREEP THAT DEVOURED THE SPRINT

In the beginning, it was a simple request. The client wanted a minor feature added to the product —something small, something easy. The team estimated it would take just a few hours. No big deal. But as the sprint went on, what started as a tiny request turned into a **monster of a project**, dragging timelines with it and leaving a trail of frustration behind.

In this chapter, we explore the nightmare of **feature creep**, how a simple change can snowball into a full-scale project, and how you can manage the ever-growing list of requests without losing your mind—or your sprint velocity.

THE INNOCENT START

It begins like this: a client reaches out with a small idea, something they believe will improve the product.

"Could we just add a toggle here for users to customize this setting?"

You look at the request, and it seems harmless enough. A toggle? Sure. A quick line of code. Maybe an extra option in the admin panel. Your developers shrug it off—this won't take long at all. You greenlight the task, slotting it neatly into the sprint.

"Easy win," you think, confidently moving forward.

But then, just as the team begins working on it, something strange happens. The client comes back with a follow-up:

"Oh, and while we're at it, could we also make it so users can configure their notifications too?"

A small add-on. Harmless, right? What's a little more customization? So, the team adjusts the plan, thinking this is still manageable. But deep down, you can already sense what's coming.

THE SNOWBALL EFFECT

Within days, the "small" request begins to balloon. More emails come in. More "small" features are added to the original task. The client starts asking for things that were never part of the original conversation:

> **"Actually, could we make that toggle integrate with the user's profile settings? And let's add the ability to generate reports from that, too."**

Suddenly, your quick win has become a **mini project**. The developers are now holding daily discussions about how this change will impact the database, the user interface, and every other part of the system. The timeline has doubled—maybe even tripled.

You know what this is: **feature creep**. And it's devouring your sprint.

THE TEAM'S GROWING FRUSTRATION

As the requests pile up, you start to notice a change in the team's mood. What was supposed to be a quick addition has now become a **time sink**. They've stopped calling it a "simple task" and are now referring to it as the "never-ending feature."

> **"Didn't this start as a toggle?"** one of the developers asks, barely masking their exasperation.

> **"Now it's a full-blown customization engine,"** another mutters.

Morale takes a hit. No one likes to see their well-planned sprint turned into a mess of last-minute changes and scope expansions. But the client keeps asking for more, and saying "no" feels harder with every request. After all, how do you stop the snowball once it's already rolling downhill?

THE ART OF PUSHING BACK

At some point, you realize something has to give. The sprint is falling apart, and the feature creep is threatening to derail everything else you've planned. It's time to have **the talk** with the client.

> **"We're happy to make these adjustments, but we need to prioritize,"** you explain gently. **"This request is starting to exceed the scope of what we can deliver in the current sprint."**

The client, of course, doesn't see the problem. To them, every new feature is critical. But you've been down this road before. You know the importance of setting boundaries.

> **"We'll break this into phases,"** you suggest. **"Let's focus on delivering the core functionality first, and we can schedule the additional features for the next sprint."**

It's a balancing act. You want to keep the client

happy, but you also need to protect your team's **sanity and velocity**.

REINING IN
THE CREEP

The client agrees to the phased approach, and the team lets out a collective sigh of relief. By breaking the task into smaller, manageable chunks, you've taken control of the **feature creep** before it completely derailed your progress. The key is communication—letting the client know that while their requests are valid, they need to be handled in a way that doesn't burn out the team or delay the entire project.

> **"We'll get the toggle done first,"** you tell the team, restoring a sense of order. **"The rest can wait."**

The developers nod, thankful that the never-ending list of requests has been tamed, at least for now.

THE SPRINT POST-MORTEM

After the sprint concludes, you sit down with the team for the post-mortem. It's time to review what went right, what went wrong, and—most importantly—how to avoid feature creep in the future.

"We need to define the scope better next time," one of the developers says.

"And make sure we have clear boundaries with the client," adds another.

You agree wholeheartedly. Setting expectations early on is key. The moment you let a "small change" turn into an avalanche of requests, you lose control of the sprint. But by being proactive, you can manage client requests while still delivering on time.

You know this won't be the last time you deal with feature creep, but at least now, the team has a better strategy for handling it.

THE OPTIMIST'S TAKEAWAY

Feature creep is one of the most common—and frustrating—challenges in tech. What starts as a simple request can quickly spiral into a mountain of additional work, leaving your team overwhelmed and your timelines in tatters. But with clear communication and firm boundaries, you can **manage expectations** and keep the project on track.

As a CTO, your job is to balance client satisfaction with realistic goals. It's about knowing when to say "yes" and when to push back—guiding the project in a way that benefits everyone involved.

Because in the world of tech, **every little feature** has the potential to become a full-fledged project. The key is to know when to **draw the line**.

CHAPTER 18:
THE VENDOR
THAT VANISHED

If there's one thing that keeps every CTO awake at night, it's the thought of a **third-party vendor** going rogue. Whether it's an essential API, a cloud service, or a critical integration, you rely on these vendors to keep things running smoothly. But when they suddenly **disappear**—no notice, no explanation—everything grinds to a halt, and you're left scrambling to pick up the pieces.

In this chapter, we explore the chaos of a critical vendor disappearing mid-project, how it sends your team into a frenzy, and how you manage to pull things together while navigating the **vendor black hole**.

THE CALM BEFORE THE VANISHING ACT

Everything was going fine. Your team had integrated a new third-party service to handle a key part of the platform. It worked seamlessly, and the project was on schedule. The vendor's API was humming along, doing its job without any hiccups. You didn't think twice about it—why would you? The vendor had been around for years and was a trusted partner.

> **"This integration is solid,"** one of the developers says confidently during the sprint review.

You nod in agreement. There's no reason to worry. You have backups for everything else, but this vendor? They're reliable. They're part of the foundation now.

Famous last words.

THE FIRST SIGN OF TROUBLE

It's a typical Monday morning. The team is starting to ramp up for the week when one of your developers sends a message that immediately raises alarm bells:

"Uh... guys? The vendor's API is down. Can't connect."

No big deal, right? It's probably just a brief outage. You've seen this before. Vendors have hiccups from time to time. You give it a few minutes, then check again.

"Still down. No response from their support team either."

Now it's getting serious. Your heart rate quickens as you try to access the vendor's website—**nothing**. Not a single response. It's like they vanished into thin air. You send an email to their support desk, only to get a bounce-back saying the **domain no longer exists**.

"Wait, what?"

This isn't a routine outage. This is a full-scale **disappearance**.

THE PANIC
SETS IN

Your team scrambles. The vendor's service was critical to the project, and without it, you're stuck. The feature you'd just spent weeks building suddenly doesn't work. It's as if the entire foundation has been ripped out from under you.

"Did we miss something? Did they send any emails about this?" one of the developers asks frantically.

You check your inbox, digging through months of communication with the vendor. Nothing. No warnings, no notifications, no sign that they were planning to shut down.

"They just... disappeared?" another developer mutters, in disbelief.

It's the stuff of CTO nightmares—relying on a vendor that vanishes without a trace. And now, you're left to figure out what to do next.

THE BACKUP PLAN THAT NEVER EXISTED

Like most tech leaders, you have **contingency plans** in place for almost every scenario. But you never expected this. How could you? The vendor was reliable—until they weren't.

"We need a backup plan," you say, scanning the room for solutions.

But here's the truth: there was no backup plan for this. The vendor was so deeply integrated into the project that removing them means rebuilding a huge chunk of the system from scratch. The team looks at you, waiting for direction.

"Alright, let's start with the basics. Find an alternative vendor and see if we can switch over without too much disruption," you say, knowing that "without too much disruption" is wishful thinking at that point.

THE SCRAMBLE FOR A REPLACEMENT

With the clock ticking, the team dives into **damage control mode**. Developers are scouring the web for alternative vendors. They're comparing APIs, pricing models, and integration times—trying to find something, anything, that will restore the broken part of your system.

> **"I found one that looks promising, but their API is different,"** one developer says, already digging into the documentation. **"We'll need to refactor quite a bit to make it work."**

You knew that was coming. No two vendors are exactly alike, and switching over will be painful. But at this point, there's no choice.

> **"Let's get started on it,"** you say, pushing forward. **"We'll refactor, test, and roll it out as soon as possible. In the meantime, keep**

trying to reach the original vendor just in case this is a temporary situation."

Though deep down, you know it's not.

THE CLOCK IS TICKING

As the hours pass, the pressure mounts. You're racing against time, knowing that every minute the system is down is costing your team valuable progress—and potentially **costing your clients money**. And it's not just about the technical switch. There are contracts, SLA agreements, and trust built on the back of that vendor's service.

Your phone buzzes with updates from the team:

> **"We're making progress, but this new vendor's API doesn't handle X the same way. It's going to take longer than we thought."**

You take a deep breath. This is the reality of tech—things go wrong, and all you can do is **adapt**. You've been through worse. You've survived system crashes, bugs that refused to die, and the dreaded midnight production outages. But something about this feels different—**more personal**. A vendor just disappearing without warning? That's a new level of chaos.

DAMAGE CONTROL WITH CLIENTS

As your team works frantically to rebuild the integration, you have to **face the clients**. You start drafting an email update, knowing you'll need to explain the situation without sending them into a panic.

> **"Dear valued client, we're experiencing a temporary service disruption due to unforeseen issues with one of our third-party vendors. Our team is working around the clock to restore functionality and ensure minimal impact to your service. We will keep you updated on our progress and notify you as soon as the system is back online."**

You hit send, hoping the words convey confidence and calm, even though inside, you're bracing for the storm of replies. You know that behind every "no problem, let us know when it's fixed" email is a client quietly thinking, **"Why didn't they have a backup plan?"**

THE LIGHT AT THE END OF THE TUNNEL

After what feels like days (but is really just one long, caffeine-fueled night), your team manages to get the new vendor integrated. It's not perfect, but it's functional. The refactoring was tedious, and some of the customization you had with the original vendor isn't available yet, but the system is **back online**.

The team lets out a collective sigh of relief. You see the exhaustion on their faces—sleep-deprived, but proud of the work they've done. They managed to pull off the impossible: recovering from a **vendor blackout** and getting the system running again with minimal downtime.

> **"We did it,"** one of the developers says, a tired smile creeping across their face.

> **"Yeah, but let's hope we never have to do that again,"** another one adds.

You laugh, but you're already thinking ahead. How can you avoid this next time? What changes need to be made to ensure you never face this kind of disaster again?

REBUILDING TRUST AND SAFEGUARDING THE FUTURE

With the system back online, you shift focus to the long-term. You hold a post-mortem with the team to discuss what went wrong and, more importantly, how to prevent it from happening again.

"We need to diversify our vendor dependencies," you say. **"We can't afford to have a single point of failure like this again."**

You start researching ways to **mitigate vendor risk**—maybe setting up multi-vendor strategies, or at least having a secondary vendor as a backup. It's more work, but after what you've just been through, it's worth it.

"Let's also implement better monitoring

for these kinds of situations. If a vendor is down for even a short time, we need to know immediately."

The team agrees, and you feel a sense of forward motion. You can't control when a vendor will vanish, but you can control how prepared you are next time.

THE OPTIMIST'S TAKEAWAY

This experience has been a reminder that in the world of tech, **nothing is ever fully under your control**. You can have the best team, the best infrastructure, and the most reliable partners, but something will always find a way to go wrong. And when it does, it's up to you to **adapt, recover, and learn**.

The vanishing vendor may have caused chaos, but it also taught your team resilience. You've faced a challenge and come out stronger, more prepared for the unpredictable nature of the industry.

Because in tech, **disaster is inevitable—but so is recovery**. And each time you recover, you're better equipped for whatever comes next.

CHAPTER 19: THE NEVER-ENDING DEPLOYMENT

Deployments are supposed to be the culmination of hard work—a smooth transition from staging to production that leaves everyone feeling accomplished. But sometimes, despite all the preparation, testing, and careful planning, a deployment turns into a **marathon**. What was supposed to be a quick push of new code becomes a long, drawn-out battle against bugs, downtime, and endless patches.

In this chapter, we dive into the **never-ending deployment**—how a simple update can spiral into an all-night affair, how the team copes with the chaos, and how you, as CTO, manage to keep spirits high when it feels like the deployment might never end.

THE CONFIDENT START

It begins with optimism. The deployment window opens, and the team is ready. The new feature has been tested to the moon and back, and everything is in place for a quick, successful deployment. Spirits are high, and someone even suggests grabbing celebratory drinks afterward.

"This shouldn't take more than an hour, max," says one of the developers.

You nod in agreement. Everything looks good, and the code has been reviewed multiple times. The staging environment held up perfectly during testing, so there's no reason to expect anything but smooth sailing.

Famous last words, as always.

THE FIRST SIGN OF TROUBLE

The deployment starts off without a hitch. The code is pushed, the servers begin updating, and for a brief moment, everything seems fine. But then, right as the system is about to go live, someone notices an anomaly.

> **"Uh... I'm seeing some weird behavior on the live site,"** a developer says, their voice tinged with concern.

It's just a minor glitch at first. Nothing major, just a small visual bug that wasn't caught in staging. No problem—it's something that can be fixed on the fly. But as the minutes pass, more and more issues start to emerge.

> **"Wait, the database isn't syncing correctly."**
> **"The new API integration is throwing errors."**
> **"The login functionality is acting weird for some users."**

And just like that, your **one-hour deployment** is starting to spiral out of control.

THE PATCHES BEGIN

As the issues pile up, the team jumps into action, trying to patch things as quickly as possible. What was supposed to be a clean, straightforward deployment has now turned into a game of **whack-a-mole**, with bugs popping up faster than they can be fixed.

> **"I'll take the API errors. You work on the database sync issue,"** you say, trying to keep the team focused.

But the more you patch, the more things break. It's like the system is **fighting back**, refusing to accept the new code. Every fix introduces another problem, and the deployment window that was supposed to close an hour ago is still wide open.

THE MIDNIGHT PANIC

By now, it's well past midnight. The team is exhausted, but the system still isn't stable. You've tried everything—rolling back changes, adjusting configurations, even rebooting the servers—but nothing seems to stick.

> **"I don't get it. This worked perfectly in staging,"** one of the developers says, their frustration growing.

You feel it too. The deployment should have been done hours ago, but here you are, still knee-deep in **error logs** and **hotfixes**. The initial excitement has long since faded, replaced by a quiet determination to **get this thing done**—no matter how long it takes.

THE COFFEE RUN

In moments like this, when the deployment stretches into the early hours of the morning, **morale becomes critical**. The team is tired, tempers are fraying, and focus is slipping. As a leader, it's your job to keep everyone motivated, even when the light at the end of the tunnel feels miles away.

> **"Alright, let's take a five-minute break. I'll order coffee for everyone,"** you suggest, giving the team a much-needed breather.

There's some grumbling, but everyone agrees. The coffee arrives, and you can see the mood lift—just a little. It's enough to get everyone back to their desks, ready for another round of **bug fixes** and **error hunting**.

THE BREAKTHROUGH (SORT OF)

Finally, after what feels like an eternity, one of the developers finds the root cause of the database sync issue. It turns out there was a **configuration mismatch** between the staging and production environments—something no one had caught during testing. It's a small oversight, but it's been causing a ripple effect throughout the entire system.

> **"I've got it! Fixing the config now,"** the developer announces, and for the first time in hours, you feel a glimmer of hope.

The fix is applied, and slowly, the system starts to stabilize. The API errors disappear, the login functionality returns to normal, and the bugs that once felt overwhelming begin to fade away.

> **"We're almost there,"** you say, your voice filled with cautious optimism.

THE FINAL STRETCH

With the system finally stabilizing, the team pushes through the final few hours. It's still not perfect—there are a few minor bugs that will need to be addressed in the coming days—but the bulk of the work is done. The deployment is **live**, and the system is functional.

It's not the flawless victory you had hoped for, but at this point, everyone is just relieved that the nightmare is over.

"Great job, everyone. Let's call it a night," you say, knowing full well that sleep will come easy tonight.

THE MORNING AFTER

The next morning, as the team regroups, there's a strange sense of accomplishment. The deployment may have been a disaster, but the team **pulled through**. They handled the chaos with grace, fixed the issues, and got the system back online.

> **"That was rough, but we did it,"** one of the developers says, a tired smile on their face.

You nod in agreement. Yes, it was rough, but these are the moments that make the team stronger. Every disaster teaches you something new, and every deployment, no matter how chaotic, is an opportunity to improve.

You take a moment to reflect on what went wrong —why the staging environment didn't match production, why certain issues weren't caught earlier—and make a mental note to address those things in the next sprint.

But for now, you're just glad it's over.

THE OPTIMIST'S TAKEAWAY

Deployments are rarely as smooth as you want them to be. No matter how much you prepare, test, and double-check, there's always the possibility that something will go wrong. But that's the reality of tech—you're always working with **unknown variables**, and sometimes those variables will throw your entire plan into chaos.

The key is to **stay calm**, keep the team focused, and push through the challenges together. Every deployment teaches you something, even if it's just how to survive a night of endless bug fixing.

Because in the world of tech, there's no such thing as a perfect deployment—just **another lesson learned**.

CHAPTER 20:
THE ENDLESS
UPDATE LOOP

If there's one thing every CTO dreads more than a deployment, it's the **endless cycle of updates** —those never-ending patches, security fixes, and minor upgrades that always seem to pop up when you least expect them. You think you've got everything under control, and then suddenly, there's a **critical update** that must be applied. Before you know it, you're stuck in an infinite loop of **updates on top of updates**, wondering if there will ever be a moment of true peace.

In this final chapter, we dive into the **update loop**—how it keeps coming back no matter how much you try to get ahead, and how you, as CTO, navigate the eternal treadmill of keeping your systems (and your sanity) up to date.

THE FIRST UPDATE: IT'S JUST A PATCH

It always starts with a simple notification. An email from a vendor or service provider, politely letting you know that a **security patch** has been released.

> **"We've identified a minor vulnerability. Please apply this patch at your earliest convenience."**

No problem. It's a quick fix, nothing complicated. You schedule the update for later in the week, confident that it won't cause any disruption. After all, this is just part of the routine. You've done this a hundred times before.

> **"This will take 10 minutes, max,"** you say, not realizing that this is only the beginning.

THE DOMINO EFFECT

The patch is applied, and everything seems fine —until the next notification arrives. Another service, another system, another patch. This time, it's not optional. It's **critical**.

> **"This patch must be applied immediately to prevent security vulnerabilities."**

You drop what you're doing and jump into action, but as you dig into the details, you realize that this update requires an **upgrade** to one of the underlying systems. And to upgrade that system, you'll need to update several other components.

Suddenly, your quick security patch has become a **multi-day project**, with dependencies stacked on top of each other like dominoes. Every update you apply leads to another update, and before you know it, the week's carefully planned tasks are completely derailed.

> **"How did we go from one patch to five updates?"** one of your developers asks,

rubbing their temples.

"Welcome to the update loop," you reply with a grin.

THE PERPETUAL CYCLE

Days turn into weeks, and what was supposed to be a straightforward maintenance task has spiraled into an **endless cycle of updates**. Every system seems to be asking for attention at the same time, and no matter how much progress you make, there's always another notification waiting in your inbox.

"Critical update required for database management."

"Security vulnerability detected in the latest API integration."

"New features available for third-party services—please update to the latest version."

It's never-ending. Just as you finish one set of updates, another round appears. The systems are running fine, but your team is starting to feel like they're stuck in an infinite loop of **upgrades and patches**.

THE FORGOTTEN FEATURES

As the update loop consumes more and more of the team's time, you start to realize something alarming: all the new features and improvements you had planned have been pushed aside. You're not innovating anymore—you're just trying to stay afloat in a sea of **maintenance work**.

> **"We were supposed to roll out that new dashboard feature last week,"** a developer reminds you.

> **"We'll get to it as soon as these updates are done,"** you reply, knowing full well that "as soon as these updates are done" is a moving target.

The new features sit on the backlog, collecting dust, while the team continues to focus on keeping the current systems up to date. It's frustrating, but it's the reality of working in tech—sometimes the **back-end work** takes over, and all you can do is manage it as best as you can.

The "Just Ignore It" Temptation

At some point, you're tempted to just **ignore** the next round of updates. After all, how critical can they really be? You've survived this long without upgrading that one legacy system—what's the harm in waiting a little longer?

But you know better. You've seen what happens when updates are ignored for too long. The **security vulnerabilities** grow, the system performance degrades, and eventually, you're faced with a much bigger problem than just applying a few patches.

> **"We can't afford to ignore these,"** you remind the team, even though everyone is tired of hearing the word "update."

They nod in agreement, knowing that **delaying the inevitable** will only lead to disaster down the road.

BREAKING
THE LOOP

After what feels like an eternity of patching, updating, and upgrading, you finally start to see the light at the end of the tunnel. The backlog of updates is clearing, the systems are stable, and the notifications are starting to slow down.

"We did it," one of the developers says, cautiously optimistic. **"We're up to date."**

You let out a sigh of relief. It's been a long, frustrating road, but the update loop has been broken—at least for now. There's a brief moment of calm, a fleeting sense of accomplishment as you prepare to refocus on the **real work**—the new features, the exciting improvements, the things that actually move the company forward.

But just as you sit down to plan the next big project, your inbox pings:

"New patch available for core services. Please update at your earliest convenience."

You shake your head and laugh. The **update loop** is never truly broken—it's just on **pause**.

THE OPTIMIST'S TAKEAWAY

The endless update loop is one of the most persistent challenges in tech. No matter how much you plan, no matter how prepared you are, there's always another patch, another upgrade, another critical fix waiting around the corner. It's frustrating, it's exhausting, and it often feels like you're stuck on a treadmill that never stops.

But the key is to **embrace the loop**. It's not something you can avoid, but it's something you can manage. By staying on top of updates, keeping your systems secure, and maintaining a balance between **maintenance and innovation**, you ensure that your team is always ready for whatever comes next.

Because in the world of tech, staying up to date isn't just a task—it's a **way of life**.

THE END (FOR NOW)

And so, as we close the book on **"Downtime Disasters: When Everything That Can Go Wrong, Does,"** you, the reader, are reminded that tech is a world full of challenges, from system crashes to never-ending updates. But it's also a world full of **resilience, creativity, and growth**.

You will face many more **disasters** in your career, but with each one, you and your team will learn, adapt, and come out stronger on the other side.

Because in the end, it's not just about solving the problems—it's about **embracing the chaos** and knowing that you can handle whatever comes your way.